THE LAW OF
DILAPIDATIONS.

THE LAW OF

DILAPIDATIONS

(MACER'S).

EIGHTH EDITION

BY

S. PASCOE HAYWARD, B.A.,

Barrister-at-Law.

This Publication is authorised by the
COLLEGE OF ESTATE MANAGEMENT
(Incorporated by Royal Charter)
as one of its series of Text Books.

London :

THE ESTATES GAZETTE, Ltd.,
33, 34 and 35, Kirby Street, Charles Street
Hatton Garden, E.C. 1.

LONDON :

PRINTED AT THE OFFICE OF

THE ESTATES GAZETTE, LTD., 33, 34 AND 35, KIRBY STREET,
HATTON GARDEN, E.C.1.

PREFACE TO THE EIGHTH EDITION.

An attempt has been made in this edition to arrange the subject matter under three distinct heads : liability arising by estate, liability arising by contract, and liability arising by statute. It is hoped that this rearrangement will enable a student rapidly to become acquainted with the fundamental conceptions of a somewhat difficult branch of the law.

The Editor is deeply grateful to Mr. B. W. Adkin, of the Middle Temple, Barrister-at-Law, and Principal of the College of Estate Management, for much valuable advice and encouragement.

S. PASCOE HAYWARD,

11, New Square,
    Lincoln's Inn.
        January, 1931.

PREFACE TO FOURTH EDITION.

My primary object in compiling the First Edition of this little work for the Press was to produce a text book which might be of assistance to students in preparing for the examinations of the Surveyors' Institution. At the same time, I ventured to hope that a reference book upon this complicated subject written in as concise a form as possible would be acceptable to the busy man of affairs, to whom the larger reference works and records of law cases might not be easily accessible. That it has become necessary to prepare a Fourth Edition is evidence that both objects have been achieved and that the work has been acceptable to the profession generally.

In preparing the Fourth Edition the whole of the matter has been carefully revised, re-written and brought up to date, while the most recent important legal decisions have been considered in the text, and some of them have been set out at length in a Compendium.

ALFRED T. MACER.

39, Cheapside, E.C.

August, 1907.

CONTENTS.

TABLE OF CASES CITED.

A.

B.

C.

DILAPIDATIONS :
LAW AND PRACTICE.

CHAPTER I.
INTRODUCTION.

IN its popular sense the word " Dilapidations " merely expresses the idea of " disrepair," that is, of injuries to buildings by acts either of commission or of omission. In this wide popular sense of the word " dilapidations " includes many injuries to property which, however interesting to the surveyor or estate agent, have no legal consequences at all. For instance, if a man owns an ancient castle in fee simple free from encumbrances, far away from the highway and his neighbour's land, the castle may be in a state of dilapidation. But as no other person has any right to the castle, or can be injured by its disrepair, the owner may do as he will with his own, and its dilapidation can have no legal effect. The dilapidated state of a building may, however, be attended by legal liability. It is the object of this book to discuss the nature and extent of this liability, and to describe the circumstances under which it arises.

An act of commission or omission which causes a building to become dilapidated involves legal liability if it falls into one or more of the following three categories :—

1. Acts of waste.
2. Acts in breach of contract.
3. Acts in breach of statute.

1. Acts of waste. Speaking generally, the law imposes on one who is enjoying property for a limited
estate (*e.g.,* for his life, or for a term of years) a negative duty not to do anything to the property which will
injuriously affect the enjoyment of those who are to
have it when his limited estate has come to an end.
Sometimes the law goes further, and imposes on a
limited owner a positive duty to maintain, preserve and
repair the property for the benefit of those who will
follow him. Failure to observe these duties gives rise
to an action for waste. Obviously, to cause or allow a
building to become dilapidated will often amount to a
commission of waste; and, as such, involve the actor in
legal liability. This liability is dealt with in Chapter II.

2. Acts in breach of contract. When buildings are
leased, or made the subject of tenancy agreements, a
contractual relationship between the landlord and the
tenant comes into existence. By the express terms of
such a contract either the landlord or the tenant may be
put under an obligation to repair the building. To
allow the building to fall into a state of dilapidation
will generally amount to a breach of this contractual
obligation and so involve legal liability. Where, in
such a contract there is no express term imposing on
one of the parties an obligation to repair, a term is implied by which the tenant is under a limited obligation in that respect. Contractual liability is dealt with
in Chapters III, IV, V and VI.

3. Acts in breach of statute. In recent years many
Acts of Parliament have been passed dealing with
housing and public health. Under these statutes an
obligation to put dilapidated buildings into a proper
state of repair has been created in many cases where
previously no such obligation existed. It will be found

that the object of most of this legislation is either to protect the health of the public, or to prevent poor-class property from degenerating into slum property, or to prevent it from causing injury to the public or to other property by collapsing. Statutory liability is dealt with in Chapters VII and VIII.

The duty of adjoining owners with regard to party walls and fences is dealt with in Chapter IX.

The liability of an incumbent for ecclesiastical dilapidations arises under special measures and is given separate treatment in Chapter X.

Chapter XI contains a brief treatment of agricultural dilapidations.

Another way in which the dilapidated state of a building may have legal consequences is when a person enters such a building, and as a result of its condition, suffers personal injury. In certain circumstances, which are described in Chapter XII, an action will lie against the occupier of the building at the suit of the person so injured.

CHAPTER II.

LIABILITY ARISING FROM ESTATE.

PART I.—THE NATURE OF WASTE.

WASTE is any injury to, destruction, or substantial alteration in character of land, buildings, gardens, trees, etc., committed or permitted, in excess of his rights, by a tenant in temporary possession of such land, etc., whereby the interest of the reversioner or remainderman is depreciated. The obligation of a tenant not to commit waste does not spring from any agreement by him to that effect, but arises from the general law of the land as an incident of the estate which the tenant holds. Indeed in many cases there is no agreement by the tenant at all. For instance, in the common case where a testator leaves land to one person for life, with remainder to another in fee simple, the former person has entered into no agreement with anybody, but nevertheless the law will restrain him from committing any acts which will substantially change the character of, or cause deterioration in the land to which the latter person will some day be entitled.

There can be no action for waste unless there is injury to the interest of the reversioner or remainderman.[1] Moreover, the injury must be substantial, a merely nominal injury does not amount to waste.[2]

Waste is of two kinds (a) Voluntary; (b) Permissive.

(a) Voluntary waste consists of acts of *commission;* as when a tenant does something which he is bound by

---

[1] *Defries* v. *Milne* (1913) 1 Ch. 96.

[2] *Harrow School* v. *Alderton* 2, B. & P. 86.

law not to do; such as pulling down a house, cutting down trees, breaking up meadow land, opening new mines or gravel pits, etc., destroying landlord's fixtures, cutting a new doorway or a window, bricking up a window opening, altering a private house into a shop, altering the level of land by depositing rubbish.[1] It is voluntary waste to pull down or remove any part of a building such as windows, doors or wainscot.

Voluntary waste may also be committed by altering the character of the property, even though such alteration improves it, *e.g.*, by adding a new wing to a house, or converting a brewery worth £120 per annum into houses worth £200 per annum, or pulling down an old house and re-building it in an improved fashion. Such waste is termed meliorating or ameliorating waste. In practice the reversioner has no remedy if meliorating waste is committed, unless he can prove injury to the reversion, which is improbable; and an injunction to restrain meliorating waste will not be granted if no injury to the reversion is threatened.[2]

(b) Permissive waste is a mere passive act of *omission*, of neglect in allowing that to happen which the tenant is by law bound to prevent; as when a tenant allows parts of a building to decay from want of paint; or to fall for want of structural repairs; or allows rain to enter through a defective roof and cause damage to the interior; or a fence to decay whereby deer in a park are dispersed; or the sea or a river wall to fall into disrepair, whereby meadows are inundated by water and become unprofitable.

---

[1] *West Ham Central Charity Board* v. *East London Waterworks Co.*, [1900] 1 Ch. 624, in which the definition of waste was discussed at great length.

[2] *Doherty* v. *Allman*, (1878) 3 App. Cas. 709; 39 L.T. 129; *Meux* v. *Cobley*, [1892] 2 Ch. 253.

A tenant's common law liability for waste does not make him liable to repair damage which is the result of an " act of God," such as earthquake, storm, lightning, etc.; nor to make good damage caused by accidental fire, but if the fire was intentionally lighted or was the result of the tenant's negligence he will be liable.

As between landlord and tenant injury to or destruction of a building, resulting from its use by a tenant in a reasonable and proper manner for the purpose for which it was let, is not waste. For example, in a case where a grain warehouse had been let to a tenant, and shortly afterwards, owing to the weight of the grain, a beam which supported one of the floors broke, and ultimately the external walls sank and bulged, it was held that the tenant had not been guilty of waste.[1]

In *Manchester Bonded Warehouse Company* v. *Carr*[2] it was said,[3] "In the absence of an express agreement to that effect, a tenant is not liable for the destruction of the property let to him if that destruction is in fact due to nothing more than a reasonable use of the property, and any use of it is . . . reasonable provided it is for a purpose for which the property was intended to be used, and provided the mode and extent of the user was apparently proper, having regard to the nature of the property, and to what the tenant knew of it, and to what as an ordinary business man he ought to have known of it."

In these cases the burden of proof is on the tenant. Prima facie the property must be restored; and, if it is destroyed, the tenant must, in order to exonerate him-

---

[1] *Saner* v. *Bilton*, (1878) 7 Ch. D. 815 ; 47 L.J. Ch. 267.

[2] 5 C.P.D. 507.

[3] At p. 512.

self, prove that the destruction was due to causes for which he was not responsible.[1]

Those acts of commission and omission dealt with above under the titles of voluntary waste and permissive waste respectively were originally the only kinds of acts which the common law would recognise as amounting to waste. So, if a testator by his will, or a settlor in a trust deed, gave land to a person for life and expressly provided that he was not to be liable for waste, *i.e.*, " without impeachment of waste," the life tenant could do anything he liked in regard to the land. He could pull down the mansion house, sow the lawns and fields with salt and cut down every ornamental or shade tree. Thus he could out of mere spite lay waste the property and make it absolutely valueless to the person who was to have the land after his life interest had terminated. The Courts of Equity, however, early decided that when the testator or settlor gave the land to the life tenant " without impeachment of waste," he did so only in order that the life tenant should have the full enjoyment of the property by felling the timber, or opening mines, or pulling down old cottages to build new ones, etc., and that he never meant the life tenant to be able to lay waste the property in this way. The Courts therefore invented the doctrine of *equitable waste*. They decided that even if a tenant were expressly made " unimpeachable for waste," this meant ordinary legal waste, voluntary or permissive; but there were some acts of destruction so extravagant or gross that it would be unjust and inequitable to allow the tenant to commit them. So in *Vane* v. *Lord Barnard*[2] the

---

[1] 5 C.P.D. at p. 512.
[2] (1716) 3 Vern 738.

defendant settled Raby Castle on himself for life without impeachment for waste, with remainder to his son for life, with remainder to his son's sons in tail. " Having taken some displeasure against his son, he got 200 workmen together, and of a sudden stript the castle of the lead, iron, glass, doors and boards, etc., to the value of £3,000." The Court granted an injunction to prevent further waste and ordered him to repair the castle. Equitable waste, therefore, means, not waste that is equitable or just, but waste that is so gross and extravagant that the Courts of Equity would restrain a tenant from committing it even although he was expressly given the land " without impeachment for " waste.

Equitable waste includes such things as pulling down the mansion house, cutting timber left for shelter or ornament, ploughing up lawns, etc.

Before the passing of the Judicature Act, 1873,[1] the Courts of Law and Equity were separate, and the Courts of Law had no power to restrain equitable waste or indeed any acts of injury at all if the tenant had been expressly made unimpeachable for waste. Courts of Equity, however, had power to do so, and as has been seen did in fact do so.

By the Judicature Act, the Courts of Law and Equity were united, and the King's Bench Division and the Chancery (the old Equity) Division of the High Court of Justice have now equal jurisdiction, and either division can restrain equitable waste, so that the distinction is no longer important, although the expression has been retained to distinguish such waste from that committed by ordinary tenants for

[1] 36 & 37 Vict., c. 66.

life or for years, who are impeachable for ordinary waste.

By the Judicature Act, 1873, Section 25 (3), " an estate for life without impeachment of waste shall not confer or be deemed to have conferred upon the tenant for life any legal right to commit waste of the description known as equitable waste, unless an intention to confer such right shall expressly appear by the instrument creating such estate." Therefore, if it is intended to give the tenant for life without impeachment of waste a right to commit " equitable " waste, it must be expressly mentioned, otherwise the Courts will restrain such waste.

PART 2.   THOSE WHO MAY BE LIABLE FOR WASTE.

(a) *Tenants at will.* If a tenant at will commits voluntary waste he thereby in effect determines his tenancy, and his landlord can bring an action against him for trespass. A tenant at will is not liable for permissive waste,[1] owing to the uncertainty of his holding.

(b) *Tenants from year to year.* A tenant from year to year is liable for voluntary waste,[2] even when it is committed while holding over after the expiration of his tenancy. The question as to whether he is liable for permissive waste is somewhat uncertain. In *Torriano* v. *Young*[3] there is a dictum to the effect that he is. On the other hand, text book writers of authority have expressed the opposite view.[4] The point is, however, of little practical importance, for in most cases where such a tenant commits what might amount to

---

[1] *Hornett* v. *Maitland*, 16 M. & W. 257.

[2] *Burchell* v. *Hornsby*, 1 Camp 360.

[3] 6 C. & P. 8.

[4] 1 *Wms. Saund*, 574 (Ed. 1 & 71).

permissive waste, he will make himself liable in contract for breach of a term to keep the demised premises
in a tenant-like manner, which as we shall see later,[1] is
implied in such tenancy agreements.

(c) *Tenants for years*.   A tenant for years almost
invariably holds under a written lease containing
covenants to repair, so that questions seldom arise as
to his liability for waste as distinct from breach of
covenant.   It must be remembered, however, that the
liability for waste is not excluded by the fact that the
tenant has entered into a repairing covenant.   The
landlord may, if he thinks fit, sue the tenant both for
committing waste and for breach of contract.   In the
majority of cases the liability under the covenant is
more stringent, and more clearly defined than the
liability for waste, and consequently it is generally
found more convenient to bring the action under the
former head.   A tenant for years has been held liable
for both voluntary and permissive waste,[2] and it seems
he is liable to his landlord, or the latter's assignee, for
waste committed or permitted by himself or by others,
and his liability will continue should he hold over after
the expiry of a notice to quit.

An assignee of a term of years is liable for both
voluntary and permissive waste to the reversioner or to
the assignee of the reversion, in the same way as the
original tenant was liable.   But after the assignee of a
term assigns his interest to another his liability as
regards any subsequent waste will cease.

(d) *Tenants for life*.   The estate of a tenant for
life usually arises under either a will or a settlement.

---

[1] See p. 24.

[2] *Davies* v. *Davies* (1888), 38 Ch. D. 499.   *Defries* v. *Milne* (1913),
1 Ch. 98.

Sometimes the testator or settlor gives express directions as to the repairs which are to be done by the tenant for life, and in such cases the extent of the liability of the tenant depends upon the directions so given. Thus in *Haskell* v. *Marlow*[1] a testator devised a dwelling house to his wife for life " she keeping the same in good condition (reasonable wear and tear excepted)." The widow occupied the house for 42 years. It was held that, having accepted and occupied the premises, she was bound by the terms of the devise, and that the question as to whether her executors were liable for the dilapidated state of the premises at her death depended upon a proper construction of the provision of the will.

If, by the terms of the will or settlement, the tenant for life holds *without impeachment of waste,* he is only liable for "equitable" waste, as already explained.

If the will or settlement expressly so provides, the tenant for life may even be allowed to commit equitable waste.

If the will or settlement lays no condition on the tenant for life as to repairs, and does not expressly make him unimpeachable for waste, at common law the tenant was liable for voluntary, but not liable for permissive waste. By Section 89 of the Settled Land Act, 1925 (replacing Section 29 of the Settled Land Act, 1882) the tenant for life of a settlement may execute any improvement authorised by the Act without being made liable for waste. The authorised improvements are set out in the Third Schedule to the Act. The most important improvements connected with existing buildings, and those which, therefore, most closely concern the subject under discussion, are contained in Part II

---

[1] (1928) 2 K.B. 45.

(iv) and (v) of the Schedule. By clause (iv) the restoration or reconstruction of buildings damaged or destroyed by dry rot, and by clause (v) structural additions to or alterations in buildings reasonably required are made authorised improvements. How far the words " reasonably required " limit the right of a tenant for life to carry out alterations in a building or make additions thereto without laying himself open to an action for waste has not yet been decided.

(e) *Copyholders*. Before 1926 copyholders were liable for both permissive and voluntary waste. If owing to their act or neglect buildings decayed, or land was flooded, etc., their tenements were legally forfeitable to the lord of the manor. Forfeiture could also be obtained for such acts as ploughing up meadows, pulling down houses, opening and working mines, or felling timber contrary to the custom of the manor. The question of liability was entirely governed by the custom of the manor.

Now by Section 128 (1) of the Law of Property Act, 1922, which came into force on January 1st, 1926, copyhold is abolished as a form of tenure.

By Section 128 (2) (c), however, rights of forfeiture (except those specified) are saved until the manorial incidents are extinguished. The right of forfeiture for waste, therefore, continues until, in accordance with Section 138 (1), extinguishment of the manorial incidents takes place. Broadly speaking, the incidents are extinguished automatically in 1935, or earlier if an agreement is made between the Lord of the Manor and the Copyholder for payment of compensation in respect of them.

(f) *A mortgagor in possession*. A mortgagor remains the owner of the mortgaged property, and while in possession he may take the rents and profits thereof without accounting. Equity, however, regards the mortgaged property as security for the debt, and will restrict the mortgagor's rights so that their exercise will not injure those of the mortgagee. On this principle a mortgagee may obtain an injunction to restrain a mortgagor in possession from committing voluntary waste, where the act complained of would depreciate the value of the security.[1]

A mortgagor in possession is not liable for permissive waste. Before 1926 mortgages were made by conveying the mortgaged property to the mortgagee, and giving to the mortgagor a right, called an equity of redemption, to have the property reconveyed on payment of the debt secured. Now, after 1925, all mortgages are carried out by a grant of a long lease of the property to the mortgagee. Both the old conveyances and the modern leases usually impose a contractual obligation on the mortgagor to keep the mortgaged property in repair, and so make him liable in contract for acts which would apart from contract amount to permissive waste.

(g) *A mortgagee in possession.* A mortgagee in possession is not liable for permissive waste. At the same time it is his duty to keep the premises in repair so far as the rents and profits in his hands will admit of, after deducting the interest to which he is entitled under the mortgage. Naturally, it is to his interest to maintain his security, but he is not bound to spend his own money on repairs. The mortgagee in possession is, however, liable for gross or wilful negligence in respect of failure to repair[2] (*i.e.*, for equit-

---

[1] *Farrant* v. *Lovel*, 3 Atk. 723.
   Robinson v. *Litten*, 3 Atk. 210.

[2] *Taylor* v. *Mostyn*, (1886) 33 Ch. D. 226.

able waste), especially when the mortgaged property is leasehold and the neglect to repair renders the lease liable to forfeiture. Thus in a case where a mortgagee entered into possession of unfinished leasehold buildings, and he neither sold the property nor completed the buildings, he was held liable for wilful neglect.[1] He is not bound to lay out money on the property except for necessary repairs.[2] He may pull down ruinous houses and build others in their stead,[3] but it is inadvisable for him to carry out substantial repairs not strictly necessary, or to make lasting improvements without the consent or acquiescence of the mortgagor. It has been held that when he has done so, and it is proved that the value of the property has thereby increased, he is entitled to be repaid by the mortgagor.[4] The improvements, however, must not be of such a character as to increase the amount of the mortgagor's debt unduly, and thus make it difficult for him to redeem. A mortgagee is not, as a matter of course, entitled to interest on the money he has expended on repairs, but in some cases interest has been allowed him on expenditure on necessary repairs and lasting improvements.

Whether the mortgagee in possession was ever liable for voluntary waste is doubtful. Freehold mortgages existing on the 1st January, 1926, were by the Law of Property Act 1925, 1st Schedule, Part VII, converted into mortgages by lease for a long term of years " without impeachment for waste." No doubt the mortgages by lease created after the Act will contain a similar provision.

---

[1] *Perry* v. *Walker*, (1855) 24 L.J. Ch. 319,

[2] *Godfrey* v. *Watson*, (1747) 3 Atk. 518 ; *Sandon* v. *Hooper*, (1843) 6 Beav. 246.

[3] *Hardy* v. *Reeves*, (1799) 4 Ves. 466.

[4] *Shepard* v. *Jones*, (1882) 21 Ch. D. 469.

PART 3. REMEDIES FOR WASTE.

At Common Law the liability for waste originally only extended to those tenants whose estates were created by operation of law, such as tenants by the curtesy, and the tenants in dower, and not to tenants for life and tenants for years, the reason being stated by Coke thus, " The law created their estates " (*i.e.*, estates of dower and curtesy) " therefore, the law gave a remedy against them ; but tenants by demise or years came in by demise or lease of the owner of the land, and he might in his demise have provided against the doing of waste by his lessee, and if he did not, it was his negligence and default." In the thirteenth century, however, two Acts of Parliament were passed which extended the liability for waste to tenants for years and tenants for life.

The Statute of Marlborough[1] enacted that : " Fermors during their term shall not *make waste* . . . without special license had by writing of covenant making mention that they may do it; which thing if they do and thereof be convict, they shall yield full damage by amerciament grievously." " Amerciament " is a fine assessed by a jury instead of being, as is usually the case, fixed by the Court or by Statute.

The term " fermors " in the above Act was held to include all those who held by lease for life or lives or for years.

The Statute of Gloucester[2] created a much more stringent remedy against those who committed waste, and expressly made it available against tenants for life as well as tenants for years. It brought into being the writ of waste, and provided that anyone found guilty

[1] 52 Henry III., c. 23, s. 2.
[2] 6 Edw. I., c. 5.

of waste in an action under the writ should forfeit his land and pay three times the value of the waste which had been committed. The procedure by writ of waste was highly technical and cumbersome, and the practice gradually grew up by which the plaintiff seeking a remedy for waste brought his action in case, instead of using the writ. The writ itself was abolished by the Civil Procedure Acts Repeal Act, 1879.[1]

The result of the foregoing is that the old writ of waste is no longer in use; but an action on the case in the nature of waste still exists and can be employed whenever it is desired to enforce a liability for waste.[2]

The remedy for waste is damages, and the proper measure of damages is the amount by which the value of the reversion has been diminished, less a discount for immediate payment. So in *Whitham* v. *Kirkham*[3] the defendant, who was holding land of the plaintiff under a lease for years, removed soil from the demised land and placed it on his own land. The cost of replacing the soil would have been £75, and in the court of first instance the judge assessed the damages on this basis, deducting £15 by way of discount in view of the fact that the plaintiff was to be compensated immediately whereas he would not feel the injury until the lease fell in. On appeal it was held that the true basis was not the cost of reinstatement,[4] but the diminution in value of the reversion. There was evidence that it would cost from £10 to £15 per acre to bring into cultivation the land from which the soil had been removed,

---

[1] 42 & 43 Vict., c. 59.

[2] See *Doherty* v. *Allman*, 3 App. Cas., 732, per Lord Blackburn.
Woodhouse v. *Walker*, 5 Q.B.D. 404 at pp. 406, 407.
Bacon v. *Smith* (1841), 1 Q.B. 345.

[3] 16 Q.B.D. 613.

[4] Compare measure of damages in action for breach of covenant to deliver up in repair, v.p. 75.

and, as the area involved was about one acre, the Court held that £10 was the amount which ought to have been awarded by way of damages.

In cases where the act of waste has been done maliciously, or with contumelious disregard of the plaintiff's rights, the Court may depart from this standard, and award by way of vindictive damages, for the purpose of punishing the defendant, a sum in excess of the damage sustained by the plaintiff.[1]

If voluntary waste is committed, the reversioner can apply to the Court for an injunction to restrain the tenant from repeating or continuing the damage complained of, and he can bring an action to recover the amount of damage which the reversion has suffered. If the damage is slight and there does not appear to be any danger of the tenant repeating the injury, an injunction will probably not be granted. But where the damage resulting from voluntary waste is of a serious nature, the Court will interfere; for instance, a tenant can be restrained from pulling down a house and building another which the landlord objects to, or from making material alterations in a dwelling-house, as by converting it into a shop or warehouse, or from ploughing up meadow land, or removing " landlord's " fixtures. No injunction to restrain permissive waste will be granted.[2]

The estate of a tenant may be made liable in an action for waste brought by a reversioner or landlord against the personal representative of the tenant provided, first, that the action is brought within six months after such personal representative shall have entered upon his office, and, secondly, that the acts of waste

---

[1] *Whitham* v. *Kirkham* (Supra) at p. 618.
[2] *Powys* v. *Blagrave*, 4 D.M. & G. 448.

were committed by the deceased tenant during the last six months preceding his death.[1]

The executor of a reversioner or landlord may bring an action against a tenant any time within a year after the landlord's death, for acts of waste committed by the tenant during the six months immediately preceding the death of the landlord.[2] Where the waste complained of is permissive, the injury to the reversion is of a continuing character. In such a case it is immaterial that nothing active was done during the six months preceding the death.

---

[1] 3 & 4 Will, IV., c. 42, s. 2 (Civil Procedure Act, 1833), *Woodhouse* v. *Walker* (1880], 5 Q.B.D. 404.

[2] *Ibid.*

CHAPTER III.

LIABILITY ARISING FROM CONTRACT.

PART 1.—GENERAL.

In the last chapter we saw how a man may become liable for the dilapidated condition of buildings independently of any contract, but as a result of the estate which he happens to enjoy in them. We turn now to a consideration of those cases in which such liability arises out of agreement. Three preliminary remarks may be made :—

(a) The kind of contract dealt with in this book is the contract of tenancy subsisting between a landlord and his tenant. It must not be thought, however, that this is the only kind of contract which can give rise to a liability for dilapidations, for whenever one man agrees with another to put or keep buildings in repair (as in the common case of a contract between a contractor and the owner of a house), a liability for breach of contract may arise, if the buildings afterwards become dilapidated. The contract between a landlord and a tenant is of great practical importance. It is also of peculiar interest, for, as we shall see later, from the fact that the contract is one between a landlord and tenant, the law implies certain obligations to repair and keep in repair which are absent in other cases. Such contracts are not, however, intrinsically different from any other contract, but are governed by those rules with regard to fraud, mistake, consideration, capacity and so on, which make up the general law of contract and may be found in any text book on the subject.

(b) The obligation to put or keep in repair (and the corresponding liability for dilapidations) may be either express or implied. The obligation is express where the parties have either verbally or in writing agreed as to how it is to be discharged and by whom it is to be borne. It is implied when the law presumes it to exist from the nature of the contract and the surrounding circumstances. It is important to remember that an implied obligation can arise only if and in so far as the subject matter of the obligation has not been dealt with by express agreement. For example, it is an implied term of a tenancy from year to year that the tenant will keep the premises wind and water tight. If in a year to year tenancy agreement the landlord expressly undertakes to carry out all repairs which may become necessary, there is no room for the implied term, for the subject matter (*i.e.*, the repair of the premises) has been dealt with by the express agreement.

(c) The terms of the agreement between a landlord and a tenant are, in the majority of cases, embodied in a lease which usually contains a covenant dealing with the obligation to repair. In such cases the nature and extent of the liability to repair depends, and depends only, upon the proper construction to be placed on the terms of the repairing covenant. The form of the words and phrases used in these repairing covenants has, as a result of the influence of the legal profession, become to a large extent stereotyped. The standard forms have on many occasions been before the Courts, and received judicial interpretation. Consequently, the rights and duties of the landlord and the tenant under them have become well defined. It is well to bear in mind, however, that contractual duties depend in each case entirely on the terms of the particular contract from which they spring. Where common forms are used the duties will be in each case more or less the same. But by using different forms of words and phrases the nature and extent of the duties can be varied indefinitely.

The implied obligations of the landlord and the tenant will be first dealt with. Their obligations under the usual forms of repairing covenants will then be discussed.

PART 2.—IMPLIED OBLIGATION OF LANDLORD.

At common law in the case of a tenancy agreement of a building or an unfurnished house there is no implied condition or stipulation that it is fit for occupation, or fit for the purpose for which it is let. Still less is there any implied term that the landlord will do anything to make the building fit for occupation, or fit to be used for any purpose. The tenant takes the house or land as it stands, with all its defects.

Neither is there any implied contract by the landlord to repair any future dilapidations that may arise. Even when the premises become dangerous or collapse altogether, or are burned down, there is no liability on the landlord to repair or rebuild. The tenant will in such cases have to continue paying rent until the end of the lease, without any deduction for the lack of repair, and he will have no remedy even if the disrepair is such that he suffers personal injuries as a consequence.[1]

In *Keats* v. *Cadogan*[2] the defendant's agent knew that the plaintiff wanted a house for immediate occupation, and also knew that the defendant's was in an unfit and

---

[1] *Norris* v. *Catman*, C. & E. 576.
[2] (1851) 10 C. B. 591.

dangerous condition. He nevertheless, on the defendant's behalf, let the house to the plaintiff, who did not
know of its condition. It was held that the plaintiff
had no redress in respect of this disrepair.

In *Gott* v. *Gandy*[1] the premises were let by the
defendant to the plaintiff on a yearly tenancy, and were
at the time of the lease apparently in good condition.
Later the chimney became dilapidated, and the plaintiff gave the defendant due notice of the fact. The
chimney fell and injured the plaintiff's goods. It was
held that the defendant was not liable either in respect
of any defects existing at the time of the lease, or for
any later dilapidations, as there was no implied warranty of condition and no implied covenant to repair.

In *Bartram* v. *Aldous*[2] the house during the term of
the lease became dangerous to health owing to a defective drainage system. It was held that the tenant had
no remedy against the landlord and was liable for the
rest of the term to continue paying the full rent. In
such a case, however, as will be seen later,[3] the local
Authority may by statutory powers compel the landlord
to rectify the defects.

If the lease expressly provides that the tenant shall
do the repairs, "fair wear and tear excepted," or
" damage by fire and tempest excepted," this does not
raise any implied covenant on the part of the landlord
to do the repairs rendered necessary by the excepted
causes.[4]

The question of how far the fact that a landlord
who has never expressly agreed to do repairs, has

---

[1] (1853) 2 E. & B. 845.

[2] (1886) 2 T.L.R. 237.

[3] See *post*, pp. 101, 102.

[4] *Arden* v. *Pullen*, (1842) 10 M. & W. 321; *Weigall* v. *Walters*,
(1795) 6 T.R. 488.

always done them, raises an implied covenant on his part to do them in the future, is open to some doubt. The best opinion is that such a course of conduct is not alone strong enough to raise such an implied covenant, for in each case the repairs may have been done merely to protect the landlord's own property. *A fortiori*, the mere evidence that other landlords of similar kinds of houses do repairs will not be sufficient.[1]

From the foregoing it will be apparent how important it is, in the absence of some express warranty by the landlord as to the condition of an unfurnished house, for an intending tenant to have the house carefully examined and reported on by a surveyor or builder, before taking it, even if in the proposed lease the tenant is not going to undertake to keep the premises in repair, as he is usually required to do. If the tenant fails to satisfy himself as to the condition of a house, he may incur most serious liabilities, especially if the proposed lease is a long one, or if the premises are old or " jerry " built.

It must be remembered first that the foregoing principles have been established by the common law, and that in a certain limited class of cases alterations have been made by statute[2]; secondly, that the landlord may, of course make himself responsible for repairs by express contract.

Where a furnished house or furnished apartments are let there is an implied undertaking on the part of the landlord that *at the time of the letting*, the premises are reasonably fit for habitation, and, if they are not so, the tenant is entitled to decline to occupy them and to

---

[1] *Nelson* v. *Liverpool Brewery Co.*, (1877) 2 C.P.D. 311.

[2] See *post* p. 98.

repudiate the tenancy. He may also recover as damages any loss he may have sustained.

This was so held in a case where, owing to defective drains, there were bad smells in the basement of a furnished house.[1] The tenant, on noticing the offensive smells, at once declined to occupy the house, and although in three weeks, the landlord remedied the defects, it was held that the state of the house at the beginning of the tenancy entitled the tenant to rescind his contract, and that he was not liable for the agreed rent.

This was also held where a furnished house was found to be infested with bugs;[2] in another case where the house was infected by measles;[3] and again in a case where, although it could not be shown that infection really still existed, there was an appreciable risk that it might.[4]

There is, however, no implied contract on the part of the landlord that a furnished house or apartments shall *continue* fit for occupation during the term of the letting, and, if they subsequently become out of repair, the tenant will not be released from his agreement.[5]

PART 3.—IMPLIED OBLIGATION OF TENANT.

As stated in a previous chapter,[6] when land or buildings are let to a tenant, it is the duty of the tenant to use and enjoy the same in such a way that the reversion is not injured; in other words, a tenant is liable for waste.

---

[1] *Wilson* v. *Finch-Hatton*, (1877) 2 Ex. D. 336.

[2] *Smith* v. *Marrable*, (1843) 11 M. & W. 5.

[3] *Bird* v. *Greville (Lord)*, (1884) 1 C. & E. 317.

[4] *Collins* v. *Hopkins*, (1923) 39 T.L.R. 616.

[5] *Sarson* v. *Roberts*, (1895) 2 Q.B. 395.

[6] p. 4.

In addition to this liability, *in the absence of any express stipulation* there is *implied* by law an undertaking on the part of the tenant to use the demised premises in a proper and tenantlike manner.

If there be in the lease an express stipulation to repair, this will govern the liability of the tenant, and the implied one to the same effect will be displaced.[1] But the implied covenant will not be displaced by an express one not to the same effect, for instance, as by one merely to *leave* the premises in a certain state of repair.[2]

The character and extent of the repairs which a tenant must carry out in order to fulfil the implied obligation has, in the case of a term of years, never been satisfactorily defined, for the reason that in such cases the obligations to repair of the landlord and tenant are almost invariably provided for by express covenants in the lease which leave no room for the operation of the implied covenant.

The question has been before the Courts occasionally in the case of tenancies from year to year. It has been laid down that the tenant from year to year must keep the premises wind and water tight.[3] He would appear to be bound to execute only such repairs as are necessary to prevent the incursion of the elements, *e.g.*, the patching up of a leaking roof so as to prevent decay of the premises. He need not effect lasting or substantial repairs such as new roofing.[4] In the case of broken glass, etc., if not broken wilfully by him, it will probably be a sufficient fulfilment of his implied undertaking, if he boards up or pastes brown paper over the

---

[1] *Standen* v. *Christmas*, (1847) 10 Q.B. 135.
[2] See *White* v. *Nicholson*, (1842) 4 M. &. Gr. 95.
[3] *Wedd* v. *Porter*, [1916] 2 K.B. 91, 100, 103.
[4] *Fergusson* v. ——. 2 Esp. 590.

broken pane, provided such methods keep out the weather. A tenant from year to year is not liable by implied contract to make good mere wear and tear of the premises.[1] In *Anworth* v. *Johnson*[2] Lord Tenderden said, " he is only bound to keep the premises wind and water tight. A great part of what is claimed by the plaintiff consists of new materials where the old are actually worn out; for that the defendants are clearly not liable." Nor is such a tenant liable to repair or rebuild if the premises are seriously damaged or burnt down by fire.[3] But he will nevertheless be liable to pay rent until the termination of the tenancy.[4]

---

[1] *Torriano* v. *Young*, 6 C. & P. 8.

[2] 5 C. & P. 239.

[3] *Horsefall* v. *Mather*, Holt N.P.C. 9.

[4] *Baker* v. *Holtpzaffell*, 4 Taunt 45.

CHAPTER IV.

LIABILITY ARISING FROM CONTRACT
(continued).

PART 1.—EXPRESS OBLIGATION OF LANDLORD.

IT is somewhat unusual for the landlord by an express provision of the lease or tenancy agreement to undertake any responsibility for repairs. Sometimes, however, he does so in short tenancies (*e.g.*, under a yearly or three years' agreement), and occasionally, although much less commonly, under a long lease. For instance, he may agree " to keep all the external parts of the premises other than the windows and doors in good repair "; and if he agrees to insure against fire he will generally agree to expend the insurance money in rebuilding.

In agreements for leases to start on a future day the landlord sometimes undertakes to put the premises in repair before that day. Should he fail to do so the tenant's rights will depend on the wording of the agreement, but generally speaking the undertaking will be treated as a promise in the nature of a condition, and on breach thereof the tenant will not be bound to take the lease.[1] When this agreement is embodied in a lease in which the tenant covenants to keep the premises in repair afterwards, the question as to whether the tenant will be held liable, under his covenant, for the non-repair of any part of the premises before the landlord has performed his covenant and put them in repair, depends upon whether the tenant's covenant is dependent on or independent of the landlord's; and this

---

[1] *Tidey* v. *Mollett* (1864), 16 C.B.N.S. 298.

depends on the language used in the covenants. So in *Cannock* v. *Jones*[1] a covenant by the tenant to keep the premises in repair "from and after " their repair by the landlord was held to be a dependent covenant, and an action brought on it by the landlord before he had performed the condition by first putting the premises in repair was dismissed. The landlord must repair the whole of the premises before the tenant can be made to repair any part.[2] On the other hand, in another case[3] a tenant agreed to keep certain farm buildings in repair and the landlord by a subsequent clause of the agreement undertook on notice from the tenant to find materials for the repairs. A barn became dilapidated and the tenant gave notice to the landlord of the fact, and asked him to find materials for the necessary repairs. The landlord failed to do so, and the tenant neglected to carry out the repairs. It was held that the tenant's obligation to repair was not conditional upon the landlord finding materials, and that the proper course was for the tenant to repair, and then claim the cost of the materials from the landlord.

An undertaking by a landlord to put premises in good tenantable repair does not import any obligation to put them in such repair as to make them fit for any particular purpose for which he knows the tenant wants them.[4]

As regards express covenants by the landlord to repair or keep in repair, the landlord's liability (if any) will depend entirely on the exact words used in the lease or tenancy agreement, and in general the landlord's covenant to repair will be construed in a similar.

---

[1] (1849) 3 Exch. 233.

[2] *Neale* v. *Ratcliffe*, 15 Q.B. 916.

[3] *Tucker* v. *Linger*, 21 Ch. D. 18.

[4] *McClure* v. *Little*, (1868) 19 L.T. 287.

manner to that of a tenant[1] in the same words with regard to the same building.[2]

There is one great difference, however, between a tenant's covenant to repair and a landlord's covenant. No matter how absolute in its wording is the landlord's covenant, no obligation arises under it until he has notice that repair is needed. That is, every express promise by a landlord to repair the demised premises must be read as if it said, "if and when the landlord has notice of any particular disrepair." This rule of law is founded on the idea that the tenant being on the premises best knows the state of their repair and so ought to give the landlord notice of it.[3] Moreover, if, apart from any express power so to do contained in the lease, the landlord entered the premises to do repairs when none were in fact needed he would be a trespasser. Notice to the landlord is necessary even where the landlord by the lease reserves a right to himself to enter and inspect the state of the premises; it is so whether the covenant is to repair the inside or the outside[4] of the premises, and in the latter case even where the disrepair can be discovered from outside the house by mere observation.[5]

In *Torrens* v. *Walker*,[6] the landlord had covenanted "at all times during the said term to keep the outside of the said premises in good and substantial repair." It was held that there was no breach of the covenant

---

[1] See Part 2, p. 36, *et seq.*

[2] See *Torrens* v. *Walker* infra.

[3] As to whether the rule applies to defects of which the tenant was ignorant, and which he could not have discovered by the exercise of ordinary care, the authorities are in conflict, see p. 99.

[4] *Ibid.* and see *Hewitt* v. *Rowlands*, [1924] W.N. 196.

[5] *Makin* v. *Walkinson*, L.R. 6 Ex. 25.

[6] [1906] 2 Ch. 166.

until the landlord had notice of the want of repair, even although he had, in the lease, reserved a right to enter and view the state of repair. In this case, the house was very old (about 200 years) and owing to natural decay it had become dangerous. But of this fact neither the landlord nor the tenant was aware. The London County Council served a notice on the landlord to remedy its condition, and on his failure to do so condemned the building and had it partly pulled down under the London Building Acts as being a dangerous structure. It was impossible to repair the building and nothing could be done but rebuild it. Applying to this case the principle laid down in an earlier one,[1] that a *tenant* under a like covenant by him "to repair" is not required to give back to his landlord at the end of the lease a different thing from that which he took when he entered into the covenant, it was held that the landlord, having only agreed to keep the outside in *repair,* was not bound to rebuild the premises and so give the tenant a new house.

The rule requiring notice to be given to the landlord has no application where the landlord demises only a portion of the premises and retains in his own control that portion which becomes defective and causes the damage.[2]

When the landlord enters into an express covenant to repair any part of the premises, the lease usually expressly gives him also a right to enter on the premises for that purpose. Even in the absence of such express provision, a landlord who has expressly covenanted to repair has an implied licence to enter on the premises and remain there for a reasonable time to

---

[1] *Lister* v. *Lane & Nesham,* [1893] 2 Q.B. 212.

[2] *Melles & Co.* v. *Holme,* [1908] 2 K.B. 100.

do those repairs.[1] On the other hand, a landlord who has entered into no covenant to repair has no right whatever to go upon the premises to inspect or to do repairs, and if he does so the tenant may treat him as a trespasser. This is so even although the result of the non-repair is to cause a forfeiture of the headlease under which the landlord himself holds.

If the landlord has entered into an express covenant to repair and after notice fails to perform his obligations, the tenant is not enabled thereby to quit the premises and treat the lease as at an end. Neither is he excused from paying rent for the period during which the premises are out of repair. He can of course sue the landlord for any damage he has sustained by the non-repair; and *prima facie* the measure of damage in such a case is the difference in value to the tenant, during the period dating from the notice of disrepair to the date of assessment of the damage, between the house in the condition in which it actually was and the house in the condition in which it would have been if the landlord on receipt of the notice had fulfilled his obligation.[2] This is not necessarily the same thing as the cost of doing the necessary repairs. Regard must always be had to the quantum of the tenant's interest in the premises. It would obviously be unjust to give to a tenant as damages the full cost of putting in repair premises of which he enjoys only a tenancy from year to year, or for a term of years which has only a short time to run.[3]

It is no answer to a distraint by the landlord for his rent that the premises are in disrepair. If a landlord who has expressly covenanted to repair, fails to do

---

[1] *Saner* v. *Bilton*, (1878) 7 Ch. D. 815.

[2] *Hewitt* v. *Rowlands*, [1924] W.N. 196.

[3] *Green* v. *Eales*, (1841) 2 Q.B. 225.

so after notice, a tenant may recover from him rent
that he has had to pay for substituted premises which
the tenant has been reasonably and necessarily
compelled to take and occupy during the time that
the original premises were untenantable. But if, after
notice of the defects, the landlord commences to repair
within a reasonable time the tenant cannot of course
charge the landlord with money which he has paid for
renting other premises during the progress of the
repairs although during that time, owing to the nature
of the repairs necessary, the premises were not safely
habitable.[1]

As has been said, the interpretation of covenants by a
landlord is similar to those by a tenant. A few of the
more important cases may be cited to show how they
have been dealt with by the courts.

In the lease of a farm for 21 years the lessee covenanted with the lessor that he would "from time to time
during the said term at his own cost (being allowed all
necessary materials for this purpose to be previously
approved in writing by the lessor and carting such
materials free of cost a distance not exceeding five miles
from the farm) when and so often as need shall require
well and substantially repair," the farm house, etc.,
belonging to the said premises. It was held that
this did not import a covenant by the lessor to supply
materials necessary for the proper repair and maintenance of the demised premises, but it only took effect
as a qualification of, or condition precedent to, the
lessee's liability to repair. " I think," said Lord Justice
Scrutton in the Court of Appeal, " sufficient meaning
is given to the words by treating them as a limitation
of the liability of the lessee . . . so that he is not

---

[1] *Hewitt* v. *Rowlands*, 1924 W.N. 135 at p. 136.

bound to execute repairs if the landlord does not previously assent to bear the cost of the materials necessary for them."[1]

In another case the tenant had agreed to take a lease of a house if the landlord would put the drains into sound and proper condition. The lease contained covenants by the tenant to pay all outgoings, and keep the premises in repair. The landlord failed to put the drains in proper condition before or after the execution of the lease, and as a consequence a nuisance from bad drainage occurred, and the landlord incurred the expense of complying with an order to abate the nuisance under the Public Health (London) Act, 1891. When the landlord sued the tenant for the cost, it was held that the tenant was not liable on the grounds (1) that the covenant to pay outgoings did not apply to a payment for work rendered necessary by the landlord's failure to put the drains in proper condition under the agreement; and (2) that the covenant to keep the premises in repair did not apply to the drains unless and until they had first been put in a proper condition by the landlord.[2]

If the landlord covenants with his tenant that he will, should the premises be burned down or damaged by fire, " rebuild and replace the same in the same state as they were in before the happening of such fire," he is only bound to restore the premises to the state in which they were when he let them, and is not bound to rebuild any additional parts which have been erected by the tenant.[3]

---

[1] *Westacott v. Hahn*, [1918] 1 K.B. 495.

[2] *Henman v. Berliner*, [1918] 2 K.B. 236.

[3] *Loader v. Kemp*, (1826) 2 C. & P. 375.

In a case where the landlord covenanted to repair and keep in repair all the external parts of the demised premises except the glass and lead of the windows, and in consequence of the adjoining house being pulled down the party wall was left exposed and without support, whereby it gave way, and the house became uninhabitable, it was held that the wall, even before the adjoining house had been removed, was an external part of the demised premises, and consequently the landlord was liable under his covenant to repair it, the external parts of premises being those which inclose them and beyond which no part of them extends.[1] The landlord had in this case refused to repair the wall, and the tenant consequently rebuilt it, and it was held that he was entitled to recover from the landlord the cost of doing so, the jury having found that this was the proper way of repairing it.

In a long lease it is not usual for the landlord to undertake any repairs, but in practice, in short tenancies, the landlord generally has to do external and internal repairs in order to preserve his property and to secure new tenants, and also because a tenant, in such tenancies will not as a rule agree to do any extensive repairs.

While dealing with express contracts by the landlord to repair, it will be convenient to consider his liability as to repairs under a representation or warranty given either by himself or his agent.

It is always advisable for a surveyor when asked by a prospective tenant as to the state of repair or as to drains, etc., to reply to such inquiries in writing, and to be careful not to give any sort of warranty without the express instruction of his principal.

---

[1] *Green* v. *Eales*, (1841) 2 Q.B. 225.

It is necessary to consider what constitutes a warranty, and what constitutes a mere representation upon the making of which the landlord incurs no liability unless it is false and made fraudulently.[1] It is often a difficult question to decide whether in a given case there has been a warranty or a mere representation, and a suggested test is whether the lessor assumed to assert a fact of which the intending tenant was ignorant, or merely stated an opinion upon the matter of which he had no special knowledge and on which the tenant might also have been expected to have had an opinion and exercised his judgment. The former case would generally amount to a warranty; but the latter would constitute nothing more than a representation. To create a warranty, no special form of words is necessary; neither need it be in writing. " It must be a collateral undertaking forming part of the contract, by agreement of the parties express or implied, and must be given during the course of the dealing which leads to the bargain, and should then enter into the bargain as part of it."[2]

Where a representation amounts to a warranty, the landlord will be liable to the tenant for damages for the breach of such warranty. In one case, for example, a tenant and landlord were negotiating for a lease, and after terms had been arranged the tenant refused to hand over the " counterpart " that he had signed, unless he received an assurance that the drains were in order. Thereupon, the landlord virtually represented that they were in good order, and the counterpart was then handed to him.

[1] *Green* v. *Symonds*, (1897) 13 T.L.R. 301.
[2] Per A. L. Smith, M.R., *De Lassalle* v. *Guildford*, [1901] 2 K.B. at p. 221.

The lease contained no reference to the drains, which were in fact not in good order. In an action brought by the tenant to recover damages for breach of warranty, it was held that the representation made by the landlord as to the drains being in good order was a warranty which was collateral to the lease, and for breach of which an action was maintainable.[1]

Where a landlord offered to let from week to week property at 9s. a week, including rates and taxes, and by a letter written at the time stated that the premises would be " clean and ready for occupation " on a certain date, it was held that the landlord was liable to the tenant for damages owing to the tenant's illness caused by drinking water stored in a dirty cistern.[2]

But a statement that a house is " well-built " is one of a very general character, and in its nature more an expression of opinion than an allegation of fact. Such an assurance is hardly likely to be looked upon by either party as a warranty.[3]

PART 2. EXPRESS OBLIGATION OF TENANT.

A tenancy agreement, especially when (as in the vast majority of cases) it is in writing, generally contains some reference to repairs, and generally casts upon the tenant some liability in this respect. The liability may amount to practically nothing or it may be very heavy.

When there is an express contract to repair, whether in a lease under seal or in a written agreement, or by word of mouth (in those infrequent cases where an oral tenancy agreement is entered into), the liability

---

[1] *De Lassalle* v. *Guildford*, [1901] 2 K.B. 215.

[2] *Stokes* v. *Gillett*, (1909) unreported.

[3] See *Kennard* v. *Ashman*, (1894) 10 T.L.R. 213, 447.

will depend entirely upon the wording of the covenant or clause, and any implied covenant to the same effect is thereby displaced.[1]

It has already been pointed out that the form of the repairing covenant inserted in most leases met with in practice is the same, and the rights and duties of the respective parties thereunder tolerably well-defined. In this part it is proposed to examine these usual forms, and discuss the rights and duties which flow from them. The following are typical examples of repairing covenants taken from actual leases.

(*a*) Tenancy at Will.—This class of tenancy seldom arises in practice, and when it does it is usually by verbal agreement. If, however, it is put into writing, the repairing contract would be very short, and the tenant would generally only agree to—

" Leave the premises in as good condition as the same are now in—reasonable wear and tear and accidents by fire explosion lightning flood and tempest only excepted."

(*b*) Weekly, Monthly and Quarterly Tenancies. —In these tenancies the tenant's liability to repair is generally very slight, and the above contract, or the following, would be suitable :—

" To keep the said premises together with the appurtenances and landlord's fixtures in good condition and so to deliver up the same on the expiration or sooner determination of this agreement (fair wear and tear and damage by accidental fire excepted)."

(*c*) Yearly Tenancies and Three Years' Agreements. The repairing covenants met with in these tenancies vary slightly, but in most cases " fair wear and tear " is excepted.

The following are a few examples :—

(1) " The tenant his executors or administrators shall and will during the period that he or they shall continue to occupy the

---

[1] *Cf. ante.* p. 20.

said messuages or premises under this agreement *keep repaired* at his or their own expense all the windows window-shutters doors locks fastenings bells and all other landlord's fixtures in upon or belonging to the said premises and *all the internal parts* thereof *and so leave the same at the end of the said term* (*reasonable wear and tear* and accidents by fire flood or tempest only *excepted*)."

(2) " The tenant shall and will *keep the interior of the said premises* and all the glass in the windows and elsewhere *in good and tenantable repair* (*fair wear and tear* and damage by accidental fire explosion storm lightning or tempest only *excepted*) and *will deliver up the same in such good and tenantable repair and condition* (*allowing for reasonable wear and tear*) together with all landlord's fixtures at the expiration or sooner determination of the tenancy and also will preserve and keep the plantations lawns garden and grounds in good order and in a proper state of cultivation and will use his best endeavours to preserve the fruit trees and shrubs."

(3) " The tenant agrees to *deliver up at the expiration* cr sooner determination *of the said term the messuage* with all fixtures attached thereto *in as good repair and condition as it now is in reasonable wear and tear and damage by* fire *excepted*."

(*d*) Leases under Seal.—In the case of a lease for a term, such as 5, 7, 14 or 21 years, it is usual for the tenant to undertake the whole of the repairs, both internal and external.

The following is a strict repairing covenant suitable for a 21 years' lease of a good class house in London, terminable (in this instance) at the end of the first seven or fourteen years :—

" AND also *will* at all times *during the said term* without being required to do so and as often as shall be necessary *repair maintain glaze pave cleanse and keep the said premises* and all erections or additions at any time hereafter to be erected thereon and all walls posts rails gates sinks sanitary and water apparatus drains pipes manholes offices and other appurtenances which shall belong to the said premises *in good substantial and tenantable repair and the same in good substantial and tenantable repair deliver up to the lessor at the expiration* or sooner determination *of the said term* AND in particular will paint with two coats at least of good oil colour and

in a proper and workmanlike manner the outside wood and ironwork of the said premises once in every three years of the said term and such parts of the inside of the said premises as are usually painted once in every seven years of the said term the last painting both outside and inside to be in the year immediately preceding the determination of this lease whether by effluxion of time or otherwise AND will at the same time with every outside painting restore and make good the outside stucco work wherever necessary and at the same time with every inside painting wash stop twice whiten or colour strip stop and repaper with paper of quality equal to the existing paper such parts of the inside of the said premises as are usually whitened coloured and papered AND ALSO will pay and contribute a fair proportion of the expenses of making repairing and securing all party and other walls gutters sewers and drains belonging to the said demised premises in common with the adjacent premises AND ALSO will permit the lessor or his agent with or without workmen and others twice in every year during the said term at convenient hours in the daytime to enter into and upon the said demised premises and view and examine the state and condition thereof and of all such decays defects and wants of reparation as shall be then and there found to give to the lessee notice in writing to repair and amend the same within three calendar months then next following within which time the lessee will repair and amend the same accordingly AND ALSO will insure and keep insured the said demised premises from loss or damage by fire in the joint names of the lessor and lessee in the
Assurance Company Limited or in some other well-established office to be approved of by the lessor in the sum of One thousand five hundred pounds at least and will pay all premiums and sums of money necessary for that purpose and will whenever required produce to the lessor or his agent the policy of such insurance and the receipt for every such payment and will cause all moneys received by virtue of any such insurance to be forthwith laid out in rebuilding and repairing the said premises and if the moneys so received shall be insufficient for the purpose will pay the deficiency out of his own moneys."

A shorter covenant suitable for a 21 years' lease would be as follows :—

" The tenant covenants to *keep the exterior and interior of the demised premises* and all additions thereto, and the boundary walls and fences thereof and the drains soil and other pipes and sanitary apparatus thereof *in thorough repair and good condition and the same in good tenantable repair and condition to yield up to the lessor* his heirs or assigns *at the end or* sooner determination *of the said term.* To paint with two coats at least of good oil paint in a workmanlike manner in every third year of the term and also in the last year thereof all the outside wood metal stucco and cement work usually painted. To paint in like manner in every seventh year of the term and also in the last year thereof the inside wood and iron and other work usually painted and also to wash stop whiten distemper strip and paper all parts now whitened distempered and papered."

(*e*) Building Lease for 99 years.—The repairing covenants are often very similar to those contained in the example given of a 21 years' lease, thus:—

" *To keep the exterior and interior of the said dwelling house when completed* and all other buildings and erections which may at any time during the said term be erected on the land hereby demised and all additions to such dwelling-house and buildings and the landlord's fixtures thereon and the yard garden walls fences drains and appurtenances thereof *in good and substantial repair and condition.*"

This would be followed by a covenant to paint the outside at stated intervals as contained in the 21 years' lease, and also a covenant to yield up in repair as before described.

(*f*) Building Lease for 999 years.—The following would be a very stringent form of repairing covenant. The tenant covenants:—

" *At all times during the said term well and sufficiently to repair cleanse uphold maintain and keep in good tenantable repair the said messuage* or dwelling-house messuages or dwelling-houses or other buildings and all additions thereto and the fixtures therein and the walls fences roads sewers drains and appurtenances thereof *with all necessary reparations and amendments* and when for that purpose the state of the premises either by decay accidents from fire or otherwise shall so require to take down the same messuages or dwelling-house messuages or dwelling-houses or other buildings and to rebuild and erect again on the said plot of land in such like good and substantial manner a similar messuage or dwelling-house messuages or dwelling-houses or other buildings under the direction of the landlord or his surveyor or agent and so that there shall always during the said term be upon the said plot of land in such tenantable repair as aforesaid good and substantial buildings of the aggregate clear letting yearly value to a good tenant or tenants of £   at the least.

" At the determination of the tenancy to yield up the said messuage or dwelling-house messuages or dwelling-houses and all additions thereto and all landlord's fixtures affixed thereto in such repair and condition as shall be in accordance with the covenants hereinbefore contained."

(*g*) **Lease of a Farm for a term of years.**—The tenant covenants :—

" To repair and keep in repair the farm-house and buildings cottages and erections on the farm and to paint paper and whitewash when necessary and from time to time to tar such wood work and coverings of buildings as may require so to be treated and to do all carting of material at his own expense, being provided by the landlord upon request with rough timber and other rough materials and lime tiles and bricks at the kiln and with paint tar and paper.

" To keep in repair all doors gates gate-irons posts rails hedges fences walls pumps stiles roads and bridges and to keep the hedges regularly brushed and trimmed and properly banked up and at proper seasons of the year to lay and plash such of them as require it and to plant young quick or thorns in the hedges where required and afterwards to properly guard and weed them from time to time and to keep the hedge bushes well faced up and backed up and not to remove fences or alter boundaries or landmarks.

" To yield up at the expiration of the tenancy all the demised premises in such a state of repair cultivation or management as shall be in compliance with the tenant's covenants hereinbefore contained.

It will be seen that the tenant usually undertakes to keep the premises in " good," " habitable," " necessary," " needful," " substantial " or " sufficient " repair. None of these expressions has any particular or technical value, and in law they all have much the same meaning. In *Anstruther-Gough-Calthorpe* v. *McOscar*[1] in the Court of Appeal, the covenant was

[1] (1924) 1 K.B. 716.

" well and sufficiently to repair, support, uphold," etc.
Bankes, L.J., said :[1] "I attach no importance to the
particular form of words used in the covenant. The
effect is the same, in my opinion, whatever words the
parties use provided that they plainly express the
intention that the premises are to be repaired, kept in
repair, and yielded up in repair." Scrutton, L.J.,
said :[2] " In my view the matter can be dealt with as if
the covenant were one ' to keep and yield up at the end
of the term in repair.' I do not think there is any
substantial difference in construction between ' repair,'
which must mean ' repair reasonably and properly,'
and ' keep in good repair ' or ' sufficient repair ' or
' tenantable repair.' " Atkin, L.J., however seemed to
take a different view. He said :[3] " I see no reason for
construing the words of covenants in leases dealing
with obligations to repair in any other way than one
would construe any other covenant. Effect should be
given if possible to every word used by the parties. It
does not appear to me useful to refer to such covenants
as the usual covenants to repair or general repairing
covenants and then consider only what is the meaning
of repair. It appears to me still less useful to take
a number of terms which may be found in different
leases, treat them all as synonymous, and so impute
to all of them a special meaning attached by authority
to one of them." The balance of authority is, however,
against Lord Justice Atkin's view, and it seems that,
while the addition of special or unusual words (*e.g.*, as
in a covenant " to keep in *perfect repair* ") may have
the effect of adding to the tenant's obligations, the

---

[1] At p. 722.
[2] At p. 729.
[3] At p. 731.

various adjectives commonly used to express the state of repair in which the tenant is to keep or deliver up the premises have little or no effect.

It may, therefore, be said that the nature and extent of the tenant's liability for dilapidations under a tenancy agreement or lease containing an ordinary repairing covenant depends upon the meaning of " repair," and the analysis of that word in *Lurcott* v. *Wakely and Wheeler,*[1] by Fletcher Moulton and Buckley, L.JJ., should be carefully studied. The former said :[2] " It is plain that the word ' repair ' refers to an operation to which the defendants (the tenants) bind themselves to have recourse. For my own part, when the word ' repair ' is applied to a complex matter like a house, I have no doubt that the repair includes the replacement of parts. Of course, if a house had tumbled down, or was down, the word ' repair ' could not be used to cover rebuilding.' " In the same case[3] Lord Justice Buckley expressed his opinion[4] that " ' Repair ' and ' renew ' are not words expressive of clear contrast. Repair always involves renewal; renewal of a part; of a subordinate part . . . Repair is restoration by renewal or replacement of subsidiary parts of a whole. Renewal, as distinguished from repair, is reconstruction of the entirety, meaning by the entirety, not necessarily the whole, but substantially the whole subject-matter under discussion."

These dicta were referred to with approval by Scrutton and Atkin, L.JJ., in *Anstruther-Gough-*

---

[1] [1917] 1 K.B., at p. 918.

[2] At p. 918.

[3] *Lurcott* v. *Wakely and Wheeler*, [1911] 1 K.B., p. 923.

[4] At p. 923.

Calthorpe v. *McOscar*,[1] Atkin, L.J., adding : " Repair . . . connotes the idea of making good damage, so as to leave the subject as far as possible as though it had not been damaged. It involves renewal of subsidiary parts ; it does not involve renewal of the whole."

A covenant to repair imports an obligation to make good damage. If the only way to make good damage to the premises is to supply certain new subsidiary parts, such as new planks in a floor, or even new walls to a building, this must be done.

Thus, in *Lurcott* v. *Wakely and Wheeler*,[2] the tenant had convenanted " well and substantially to repair and keep in thorough repair and good condition " the demised premises, and at the end or sooner determination of the term to yield up the same to the lessors, their heirs and assigns.

Shortly before the expiration of the lease the London County Council served a " dangerous structure notice " on the owners and occupiers requiring the front external wall of the house to be pulled down, it being in such a condition, owing to the effect of time and the elements (the house being over 200 years old), that it could not be patched up so as to answer the purposes of a wall.

The landlord complied with the notice, and rebuilt the wall. He then brought an action against the tenants for the costs, and was successful. The tenants appealed.

In the Court of Appeal judgment was also given in the landlord's favour, it being held that the tenant was liable to rebuild the wall in question under his repairing covenant. In the opinion of the Master of

[1] (1924) 1 K.B. 716.
[2] [1911] 1 K.B. 905.

the Rolls this portion of the wall in front was plainly merely a subsidiary portion of the demised premises, the rebuilding of this part leaving the rest of the building, going back 140 feet, untouched. The rebuilding of this wall did not change the character or nature of the building, and he was unable to see that the case was any different from one in which say, by reason of the elements and lapse of time, some rafters in a roof had become rotten and a corner of the roof gave way, so that the water came in, in which case the tenant would obviously be liable to repair under his covenant.

Lord Justice Fletcher Moulton said " We must bear in mind that while the age and the nature of the building can qualify the meaning of the covenant, they can never relieve the lessee from his obligation. If he chooses to undertake to keep in good condition an old house, he is bound to do it whatever be the means necessary for him to employ in so doing. He can never say : ' The house was old, so old that it relieved me from my covenant to keep it in good condition.'

" If it was so old that to keep it in good condition would require replacement of part after part until the whole was replaced—if that was necessary—then, by entering into a covenant that he would do it, he took on his own back the burden of doing it with all that this duty might entail."

On the other hand, where it is impossible to reinstate the building without making it, or some substantial part of it, quite different from what it originally was, the tenant will not, under a covenant to repair, be liable for the reinstatement. So in *Parkes' Drug Stores, Ltd.* v. *Edwards*,[1] the premises, which were

---

[1] Reported in *Journal of Surveyors' Institute*, October, 1923 ; p. 200.

between 80 and 90 years old, had been very badly built. Owing to the bad construction and bad materials, and without any fault of the tenant, the building developed a bulge in the front wall, and soon afterwards a considerable portion of that wall fell. In order to reinstate the building it was necessary to tear down the remainder of the front wall and the whole of one of the side walls and rebuild them. They could not, according to the present building regulations, be built in the way they had originally been. They had to be built in a different way and made much better walls. The tenant, under the general form of repairing covenant, was held not liable for this rebuilding. Had it been possible to build the new walls in the same way as the old walls, and with similar materials, no doubt the decision in this case would have been the other way. As it was, the reinstatement would have resulted in the landlord obtaining premises quite half of which were in a fundamental respect different from those demised.

Again, in *Lister* v. *Lane and Nesham*[1] the tenants under a seven years' lease covenanted that they would " When and where and as often as occasion shall require well sufficiently and substantially repair uphold sustain maintain . . . amend and keep " the demised premises, and the same " so well and substantially repaired upheld supported sustained maintained . . . amended and kept " at the end of the term yield up to the lessors.

The house was at least 100 years old, and possibly much older. Before the end of the lease one of the walls of the house was bulging outwards, and after the end of the lease the house was condemned by the district surveyor as a dangerous structure and was

---

[1] (1893) 2 Q.B. 212.

pulled down. The landlord claimed from the tenants the cost of rebuilding the house, which he alleged was necessary, owing to the tenant's neglect to repair in accordance with a notice to repair which had been served on them under the above covenant. The tenants had executed the repairs included in the notice, except to the bulged wall, the repair of which would have been impossible without pulling down and rebuilding the whole house, since the whole house had been built on a timber sill or platform resting on a muddy soil, and this platform had decayed and caused the house to sink. The house could not have been repaired by putting a new timber foundation, but it would have been necessary to " underpin " with concrete or brickwork through 17 feet of mud in order to reach the solid gravel beneath. The tenants in their defence stated that the notice to repair required work to be done which they were not bound to do by the terms of the repairing covenant and that the premises had been repaired and delivered up in repair in accordance with that covenant. The evidence given by the tenants at the trial was directed to show that the house as repaired was a house in poor condition, because it was a house with very poor foundations, and that the notice had called upon them to support the house on foundations of a totally different type from those which it had at the time when the lease began. Judgment was given in favour of the tenants, and the landlord appealed.

The Court of Appeal upheld the decision of the Court below. Lord Esher said: " If a tenant takes a house which is of such a kind that by its own inherent nature it will in course of time fall into a particular condition, the effects of that result are not within the tenant's covenant to repair. However large the words of a

covenant may be, a covenant to repair a house is not
a covenant to give a different thing from that which
the tenant took when he entered into the covenant.
He has to repair that thing which he took; he is not
obliged to make a new and different thing, and moreover, the result of the nature and condition of the house
itself, the result of time upon that condition, is not a
breach of the covenant to repair."

Lord Justice Kay agreed that in this case the underpinning would involve making an entirely new and
different house. He added : " The only way to repair
it (the house) is by this underpinning. That would
not be either repairing, or upholding, or maintaining
such a house as this was when the lessee took it, and
he is not liable under his covenant for damage which
accrued from such a radical defect in the original
structure."

So, in the case of *Wright* v. *Lawson*[1] the tenant
covenanted to " substantially and effectually repair
uphold and maintain . . . the premises " and also at
the end of the term to deliver up the premises in a
condition in accordance with the covenant. On the
first floor there was a bay window which developed
cracks, and subsequently the tenant was served with a
" dangerous structure notice " by the district surveyor
under the London Building Acts with reference to the
external walls and the bay window. The tenant
instructed his builder to comply with the notice,
and the window was taken down. As it was impossible, owing to the house being old and badly
built to re-erect the window in the same way in which
it was before, without its being again condemned as

---

[1] [1903] W.N. 108 ; 19 T.L.R. 510.

dangerous by the County Council, the tenant built a new window set back in the main wall of the house. The landlord brought an action to compel the tenant to restore the premises to the condition in which they were when the lease was granted, by replacing the bay window. The evidence showed that a bay window, such as would satisfy the requirements of the County Council, could only be erected by supporting it by two columns from the ground to the window; or at any rate, that supports of a substantial character would be required.

Mr. Justice Kekewich gave judgment for the tenant. He held that the tenant was not liable to replace the bay window, since it was impossible to do so consistently with the requirements of the London County Council. He did not think that erecting a new bay window supported by columns could be regarded as the repair of the old bay window. It would be erecting a new bay window of a totally different character. The tenant had really been prevented from performing his covenant by *vis major* in the shape of the London County Council. This decision was upheld by the Court of Appeal.

It will be noticed that in the three preceding cases the repairs would have necessitated the tenant giving to his landlord something of an entirely different character from that which he took at the date of the lease, and consequently the tenant was not liable. Where, however, a tenant had undertaken to repair, and, owing to age and the effect of the elements, to do so would involve renewal of or rebuilding a part of the premises, then the tenant would be bound by his covenants to renew or rebuild to that extent.

Referring to *Lister* v. *Lane and Nesham*[1] in his judgment in *Lurcott* v. *Wakely and Wheeler*,[2] Fletcher Moulton, L.J., said :[3] " It (*Lister* v. *Lane*) certainly contains nothing which says that a covenantor is in any way relieved from the burden of his covenant because it may be that in order to fulfil it he will have, to a certain extent, to rebuild the premises."

In the last three cases, in which the tenant was held not to be liable, the dilapidation was the result of inherent defects in the building itself, defects not discoverable by the tenant. Had the dilapidation been caused by the neglect of the tenant, the decisions would have been the other way. In *Parkes' Drug Stores, Ltd.* v. *Edwards,* Sterndale, M.R., said : " I wish to say at once that I give no countenance to the suggestion that a tenant may neglect to repair for so long that the building tumbles down, and that he may then say, ' Now this is rebuilding, and I am not bound to do it.' I do not think that anyone would listen to such a case for a moment. But it does not arise here."

These cases appear to establish the following negative proposition :—

Where the dilapidated state of a building cannot be remedied by the mending or patching of faulty parts, or by the renewal or replacement of ruinous or worn out parts, but can only be dealt with by the substitution of something entirely different from what was in existence before the building became dilapidated the tenant is not, under an ordinary covenant to repair, liable for the dilapidations, unless the state of affairs has been brought about by his neglect or default.

---

[1] *Supra.*
[2] (1911) 1 K.B. 913.
[3] At p. 922.

Assuming that a dilapidated building can be repaired without making it into something essentially different from what it originally was, the tenant under an ordinary repairing covenant is obliged to execute the repairs. The amount and the quality of the work he will be called upon to do in order to discharge his obligations will vary with the facts in each case. Obviously the tenant of a new house in Mayfair must be under a more extensive liability than the tenant of an old house in Brixton, although the wording of the covenant is in each case the same. What are the considerations which determine how much and what quality of work a tenant must do in order to repair a building within the meaning of an ordinary covenant to repair? The answer to this question, at any rate as far as a house is concerned, is to be found in the case of *Proudfoot* v. *Hart*[1] as explained in *Anstruther-Gough-Calthorpe* v. *McOscar*.[2]

In *Proudfoot* v. *Hart*,[1] the Court of Appeal was called upon to construe a three years' tenancy agreement, under which the tenant agreed " to keep the said premises in good tenantable repair and so leave the same at the expiration thereof."

The house in question was situated in Kentish Town, London, and the landlord claimed, and the Official Referee awarded, the cost incurred by the landlord after the termination of the tenancy, in repapering walls, where the paper which was upon them when the tenancy commenced had become worn out; in repainting the internal woodwork where the paint which was on such wookwork when the tenancy commenced had worn off; in whitewashing and cleaning the staircase

[1] (1890) L.R. 25 Q.B.D. 42.
[2] (1924) 1 K.B. 716.

and ceilings; and in replacing with a new floor a
kitchen floor which was in existence when the tenancy
commenced.

Against this award the tenant appealed, contending
that the Official Referee had improperly charged him
with merely decorative repairs.   The Court of Appeal
laid down the principles which ought to have guided
the Referee in deciding the extent and nature of the
repairing work the tenant ought to have done; and, as
it did not appear that he had adopted these principles
the case was remitted to him for reconsideration.

Esher, M.R., said:[1] "Good tenantable repair is such
repair as, having regard to the age, character and
locality of the house would make it reasonably fit for
the occupation of a reasonably-minded tenant of the
class who would be likely to take it. The age of the
house must be taken into account, because nobody
could reasonably expect that a house 200 years old
should be in the same condition of repair as a house
lately built; the character of the house must be taken
into account, because the same class of repairs as would
be necessary to a palace would be wholly unnecessary
to a cottage; and the locality of the house must be
taken into account, because the state of repair necessary for a house in Grosvenor Square would be wholly
different from the state of repair necessary for a house
in Spitalfields. The house need not be put into the
same condition as when the tenant took it; it need not
be put into perfect repair . . . I agree that a tenant
is not bound to re-paper simply because the old paper
has become worn out, but I do not agree with the view
that under a covenant to keep a house in tenantable

---

[1] 25 Q.B.D. at p. 52.

repair the tenant can never be required to put up a new paper. Take a house in Grosvenor Square: if when the tenancy ends the paper on the walls is merely worse than when the tenant went in, I think the mere fact of its being in a worse condition does not impose upon the tenant any obligation to re-paper under the covenant, if it is in such a condition that a reasonably-minded tenant of the class who takes houses in Grosvenor Square would not think the house unfit for his occupation. But suppose the damp had caused the paper to peel off the walls and it is lying upon the floor, so that such a tenant would think it a disgrace, I should say, then, that the tenant was bound, under his covenant to leave the premises in tenantable repair, to put up a new paper. He need not put up a paper of a similar kind—which I take to mean equal value to the paper which was on the walls when the tenancy began. He need not put up a paper of a richer character than would satisfy a reasonable man within the definition."

With regard to the tenant's obligation to paint, Lord Esher held[1] that—" If the paint is in such a state that the woodwork will decay unless it is repainted, it is obvious that the tenant must repaint. But I think that his obligation goes further than that. A house in Spitalfields is never painted in the same way as one in Grosvenor Square. If a tenant leaves a house in Grosvenor Square with painting only good enough for a house in Spitalfields, he has not discharged his obligation."

On the same principle Lord Esher held that the tenant was not bound to whitewash the ceilings if they

---

[1] At p. 54.

were sufficiently clean to satisfy a reasonable tenant, and in no case would this covenant extend to re-gilding an ornamental ceiling.

Dealing with the question of a new floor which the landlord claimed, Lord Esher said—[1]

" The question is, what is the state of the floor when the tenant is called upon to fulfil his covenant? If it has become perfectly rotten he must put down a new floor, but if he can make it good . . . he is not bound to put down a new floor. If he leaves the floor out of repair when the tenancy ends, and the landlord comes in, the landlord may do the repair himself and charge . . . the tenant with the necessary cost of a floor which would satisfy a reasonable man taking the premises. If the landlord puts down a new floor of a different kind he cannot charge the tenant with the cost of it."

The principle laid down in the above case is that the tenant must under an ordinary repairing covenant put or keep or deliver up (as the case may be) the premises in such a condition as to satisfy a reasonably-minded tenant of the class who would be likely to take them, having regard (i) to the age; (ii) to the character; and (iii) to the locality, of the property.

This principle has been followed in subsequent cases,[2] and was regarded as of universal application until 1923 when the case of *Anstruther-Gough=Calthorpe* v. *McOscar* was decided and a very important qualification was made in its operation.

The house in question in that case was one in Gray's Inn Road, and was at the beginning of the tenancy

---

[1] At p. 55.

[2] See *Evans* v. *Shotton*, [1918] W.N. 201 ; 119 L.T. 233.

just newly built. It was let as long ago as March 2nd, 1825, on a 95 years' lease. The lease contained a covenant by the Lessee " well and sufficiently to repair." At that time Gray's Inn Road was an aristocratic neighbourhood, but when the lease came to an end in 1920 the character of the locality had completely changed, and the only tenants likely then to take the house were persons of the working classes who would take the houses separately or only part of a house for short terms on weekly, monthly or quarterly tenancies, who would not accept any repairing obligations and whose requirements in the way of repair would be very moderate indeed. The question of dilapidations was referred to an arbitrator.

The arbitrator assessed the tenant's liability according to two different standards, and stated a case for the opinion of the court as to which of the two was correct. According to the first standard the tenant was under an obligation " to put the premises into such a condition as they would have been in had they been managed by a reasonably-minded owner having full regard to the age of the buildings, the locality, the class of tenant likely to occupy them, and the maintenance of the property in such a way that only an average amount of annual repair would be necessary in the future." The cost of repairs necessary if this standard was to be applied amounted to £586, and the landlord contended that this was the correct measure of the tenant's liability. According to the second standard the tenant was under an obligation only to put the premises in such a state of repair as would " satisfy the literal requirements of reasonably-minded tenants of the class now likely to occupy them . . . such repairs would not include many necessary for the maintenance of the structure according to the first standard the neglect of which, however, would not (i) interfere with the immediate comfort of the occupier . . . or (ii) cause danger to health and so come within the purview of the local authorities.'' According to this standard the liability amounted to £220, and the tenant contended that this was correct. The second of these standards is that laid down in *Proudfoot* v. *Hart* (*supra*). The Court of Appeal, however, rejected it, and adopted the first. They held that the requirements of a tenant likely to occupy the premises at the end of a lease can form a test of liability under a repairing covenant only in cases (like *Proudfoot* v. *Hart*) when the term of the lease is short, and there is no evidence that the class of tenant likely to occupy the premises has altered during its currency.

Bankes, L.J., said[1]—

'' In my opinion, the case of *Proudfoot* v. *Hart* (*supra*) laid down no rule of general application. The language used by the Lords Justices is quite appropriate to the facts of that case and must, I think, be read as applicable to those facts and to similar facts only. To extend it, as was done by the learned Judge in the Court below and has been done in many other cases, is . . . in my opinion, to misapply it. . . . In construing the covenant in the present case, or any other covenant, it is material to see what the subject-matter was which the parties had in their contemplation when the covenant was entered into (per Mr. Justice Willes in *Heffield* v. *Meadows,* L.R., 4 C.P., 595). Here there is no doubt as to the subject-matter. It was the three houses described in the lease, and the obligation undertaken was the repair of those houses. How can the extent of

---

[1] (1924) 1 K.B. at p 726.

such an obligation be measured by the requirements of the class of tenants who happen to be occupying the premises 90 years afterwards? *Proudfoot* v. *Hart* (*supra*) did not, in my opinion, lay down any such rule. When the facts of that case are looked into it is manifest that the Lords Justices who decided the case had no such question in their minds. What they were dealing with, and all that they were dealing with, was a three years' agreement for a tenancy, in which case the class of tenant at the end of the tenancy was, in their view, no doubt the same class as the class of tenant at the commencement. Upon that assumption only is the rule which was laid down by Lord Justice Lopes and which was accepted by the Master of the Rolls, in my opinion, explainable or understandable."

Atkin, L.J., said:[1] " *Proudfoot* v. *Hart* binds me to hold that it " (*i.e.,* the tenant's liability) " has reference to the reasonable requirements of a tenant of the class who would be likely to take it. Accepting that construction I have no doubt that the requirements of such a tenant are deemed to continue the same during the term, or, if not, are to be estimated by the requirements of such a tenant as would be likely to take the premises at the commencement of the term."

Having imposed this important restriction on the application of the principle laid down in *Proudfoot* v. *Hart,* the Court proceeded to adopt the first standard suggested by the Referee.

Bankes, L.J., said,[2] " provided the age of the buildings is regarded as the dominant feature, and the locality and class of tenant is only taken into account

---

[1] At p. 733.
[2] At p. 728.

in relation to, or as a consequence of the age of the buildings, I consider the rule laid down . . . a good working rule of general application."

Scrutton, L.J., said,[1] " The statement by the arbitrator " (i.e., the statement of the first standard) " is accurate, but must be limited to the condition at the time of the demise." By ' condition ' the learned judge no doubt meant the locality and the class of tenant likely to occupy the premises. The age of buildings as a condition in this connection means the age at the time when repairs become necessary and not the age at the time of the demise.

In many of the repairing covenants in common use the tenant is exempted from liability for dilapidations caused by " fair wear and tear " or " reasonable wear and tear."[2] The exact amount of protection afforded to the tenant by an exception of this kind was considered in the recent case of *Haskell* v. *Marlow*.[3] In that case a testator devised a house to his wife for life, " she keeping the same in good repair and condition (reasonable wear and tear excepted)," and after her death to his children. The widow occupied the house for 42 years. She did nothing actively to injure the house, but nothing substantially to counteract the natural process of decay. The trustees of the will claimed from the defendants, the widow's executors, the cost of the necessary repairs. The executors contended that the dilapidations had been caused by reasonable wear and tear within the meaning of the exception, and that they were consequently not liable. The Court held first that conditions of this kind in a will impose an obligation

[1] At p. 731,

[2] See examples pp. 38, 39.

[3] (1928) 1 K.B. 45.

on a devisee who accepts the gift to observe the conditions, and that such conditions must be interpreted in
the same way as covenants in a lease or tenancy agreement. It was further held that in leases, settlements
and wills the exception of " reasonable wear and tear "
operates to exempt the devisee (or tenant) from liability
for only those dilapidations, caused by wear and tear
which are reasonable both in character and amount; that
here the wear and tear, although reasonable in character,
was wholly unreasonable in amount; and that consequently the tenant was liable. Salter, J., said :[1] " To
bring dilapidations within the protection of such an
exception . . . two things must be shown : First that the
dilapidations . . . were caused by normal human use
or by the normal action of the elements, and, secondly,
that they are reasonable in amount having regard to
the contract to repair . . . and the other circumstances of the case." The learned Judge said that on
the facts before him the dilapidations, although caused
by normal human use and the normal action of the
elements, were outside the protection of the exception
because they were unreasonable in amount. In *Terrell
v. Murray*[2] the lessee covenanted to deliver up the
premises in as good repair as they were at the date of
the lease, reasonable wear and tear excepted. It was
held that the tenant was not liable for painting outside
woodwork, for repointing brickwork and for repairing
parts of a floor which had become affected by dry rot.
The learned judge said that the exception covered
dilapidations caused by friction, by exposure and by
ordinary use. In this case there was no evidence that
the amount of the disrepair was unreasonable. Indeed,

---

[1] At p. 56.
[2] 17 T.L.R. 570.

in the case of short terms it is difficult to see how wear and tear which is reasonable in character can become unreasonable in amount.

The result of the various decisions appears to be this :—

1. Where a tenant has expressly covenanted to repair he is liable to repair, and if necessary renew or rebuild any *subsidiary part* of the premises damaged by the effect of time, weather, or other causes.

2. But when the damage is of such a nature that to remedy it would result in the landlord receiving at the end of the lease a new building, or one of an entirely different character, or one of which a portion is of an entirely different character from that which was the subject of the lease, then the tenant is not liable, under his repairing covenant, to renew or rebuild.

3. It seems that in most cases a covenant to keep and to deliver up premises in " good " or " tenantable " repair is really all that is necessary to safeguard the interests of the landlord. The use of such expressions as " uphold," " maintain," " sustain," " support," " thorough repair," " substantial repair," etc., carry little or no weight in defining the extent of the tenant's obligation to repair.

4. The amount of the repairs which must be done under such a covenant is the amount which will put the building in a condition in which it will require only an average amount of annual repair in the future having regard to its age and (according to Scrutton, L.J.) also having regard to the locality and the class of tenants likely to occupy it at the beginning of the term.

5. Where there is no evidence that the class of tenant likely to occupy the premises has changed during the

currency of the term (as is often the case in short leases) the amount of repairs called for by the covenant can be estimated by the requirements of a reasonably-minded tenant of the class likely to occupy the premises at the end of the term.   *Proudfoot v Hart 1890*

6. Where the covenant contains an exception of ordinary wear and tear, the tenant is not liable for dilapidations caused by normal user or normal action of the elements, provided the amount of such dilapidations is reasonable. What is reasonable depends on the circumstances of each case. For example, if a tile falls off a roof, the tenant would not be liable for the immediate consequences; but, if he does nothing, and water gets in which causes the roof and walls ultimately to decay, such damage, although caused originally by fair wear and tear would not be within the exception because it would certainly be unreasonable in amount.   *Marshall v Mealon 1928*
Terrell v Mary

CHAPTER V.

LIABILITY ARISING FROM CONTRACT
(continued).

WE must now discuss how far and in what circumstances persons other than the original landlord and tenant can become contractually liable for dilapidations of the demised premises. The subject may be treated under two heads :—

(1) The effect of assignment by the tenant of his interest; and

(2) The effect of assignment by the landlord of his interest.

(1) The tenant, after assignment, remains liable on all *express* covenants, including an express covenant to repair, contained in the original lease, and he may be sued by the landlord on them.

The assignee of a tenant is liable to the landlord, on certain *express* covenants if such covenants " run with the land." In order that an express covenant shall run with the land, 'such covenant must *touch and concern the thing demised,* and it is sometimes a question of difficulty to decide whether or not a particular covenant does so. It has, however, been held that express covenants to repair, to put in repair, to leave in good repair, to paint, and to insure buildings against fire, are all covenants which touch and concern the thing demised, and therefore run with the land, binding the assignee even though the tenant has only covenanted for himself and did not in the lease specifically bind " his assigns."

Before 1926 this did not apply to things not in existence at the time when the lease was made; *e.g.*, a covenant to put up a building subsequently did not bind an assignee unless " assigns " were specially included in and bound by the covenant.[1] But a covenant to repair the messuage *and all other erections and buildings which should or might be erected during the term,* was held to run with the land, and bind the assignee, although " assigns " were not mentioned in the covenant,[2] the Court holding that this was not a covenant absolutely to do a new thing, but to do something conditionally, viz., if there are new buildings, to repair them. The distinction is a narrow one, and the rule upon which it is founded has been adversely criticised.[3] Moreover, it is not of much practical importance, as " assigns " are almost invariably included in such covenants.

With regard to covenants made after 1925 it is provided by the Law of Property Act, 1925,[4] that a covenant relating to any land of the covenantor or capable of being bound by him shall, unless a contrary intention is expressed, be deemed to be made with the covenantor on behalf of himself, his successors in title and the persons deriving title under him or them and subject as aforesaid shall have effect as if such successors and other persons were expressed. This extends to a covenant to do some act relating to the land notwithstanding that the subject matter may not be in existence when the covenant is made.

---

[1] *Spencer's Case,* (1583) 1 Smith, L.C. ; 5 Co. Rep. 16.

[2] *Minshull* v. *Oakes* (1858) 27 L.J. Ex. 194.

[3] See Observations of Sargant, J., in *re Robert Stephenson & Co., Ltd.,* [1915] Ch. p. 807.

[4] Section 79.

No action for breach of covenant can be brought against any assignee of the tenant, except for breaches happening while he is assignee. Therefore, by assigning even to a pauper, an assignee may get rid of his future liability to the landlord. Suppose, therefore, that A leases a house to B for a term of seven years, and suppose that after two years B assigns the remainder of the lease to C, and that after a further two years C assigns to D. B, the original tenant, is liable to A on the covenants contained in the lease during the whole seven years. There is what is often called " privity of contract " between them all the time. C's position is different. He has made no contract with A, and cannot, therefore, be made liable to him by virtue of any privity of contract. When, however, he takes an assignment from B he becomes A's tenant in place of B, and what is known as " privity of estate " exists between them. As long as this privity of estate lasts, C is liable to A on the covenants in the lease, which run with the land. But as soon as C assigns to D privity of estate between A and C comes to an end and with it C's liability on the covenants. Privity of estate then springs up between A and D, and D is liable on the covenants.

The assignee will remain liable to his immediate assignor on any express covenants which may be contained in the deed of assignment. Before 1926 it was customary to insert in assignments a covenant that the assignee and persons deriving title from him would observe all the lessee's covenants in the head lease, and the assignee would indemnify the assignor against all proceedings brought against him in respect of any breach thereof. In such cases, if A leased to B, and B assigned to C and C to D, and if D broke the repairing covenant, and if A sued B for the breach, B could claim an indemnity from C, and C from D under the express provisions of the respective assignments. Now by Section 77 (1) (c) and Second Schedule, Part IX. of the Law of Property Act, 1925, in all assignments for valuable consideration a covenant to indemnify of the kind referred to above is implied.

The assignee of a tenant may sue the landlord on such covenants contained in the lease as "run with the land." We have already seen that repairing covenants have been held to run with the land. Consequently, if the lease or agreement happens to cast upon the land-lord an express liability to repair an assignee from the tenant may enforce the covenant.

We have seen that when a tenant enters into an *express* covenant with regard to repairs, he remains bound by that covenant and liable to pay damages for its breach not only during the time that he still retains the tenancy created by the lease, but also after he has assigned the whole of his interest in the tenancy to an assignee. He is liable because his " privity of con-tract " still continues, although the " privity of estate" has come to an end. The contrary, however, is true of a tenant's implied undertakings with regard to repairs. They cease to bind him personally on the determination of the privity of estate by assignment of the term.

On the other hand, they will, as in the case of express covenants, bind the assignee to whom the tenant assigns, and such assignee will be liable to forfeiture of his estate or to pay damages if he does not keep the premises in the same repair as the original tenant was bound to do.

(2) The effect of assignment by the landlord of his interest.

With regard to leases made before 1882 the general rule is that the assignee from a landlord enjoys the same rights to sue on covenants contained in leases as had the landlord himself, provided that the lease is under seal, or the landlord is in a position to insist on a lease under seal being executed. This rule is subject to several important exceptions, an examination of which is rather beyond the scope of this book.

To leases made after 1881 the Conveyancing Act[1] of that year applies. The general effect of that enactment is to abolish the exceptions referred to above. The position now may be stated thus. The assignee of a landlord may sue the tenant on a repairing covenant provided the covenant is contained in a lease under seal or in writing. He cannot, however, sue on stipulations contained in verbal tenancy agreements, unless the agreement is such that the landlord can call upon the tenant to execute a written lease.[2]

In the same way a tenant can sue the assignee of the landlord for breach of express repairing covenants. The same distinction must be drawn between leases created before 1882, and those made after 1881, and the same rule as to verbal agreements applies in this case.

In cases where there is an implied duty on the landlord or the tenant to repair, an assignee of the landlord takes the reversion subject to the liability or with the right to enforce it as the case may be. Thus in *Wedd* v. *Porter*,[3] one Butt, the owner of certain land, leased it on September 29th, 1892, to two persons named Porter on a lease from year to year at a certain rent but without any express terms as to repairs. In 1911 Butt

---

[1] Re-enacted by Law of Property Act, (1925) Sect. 141.

[2] *Blane* v. *Francis*, (1917) 1 K.B. 252.

[3] [1916] 2 K.B. 91

died, and on December 3rd, 1912, Butt's executors conveyed the land to Wedd, the plaintiff in this case. On
September 29th, 1913, the lease came to an end in consequence of a notice to quit previously given. Wedd
then sued the Porters in respect of the dilapidations.
It was held that the Porters as tenants were under an
implied covenant to keep the buildings wind and
weather tight; that these implied covenants ran with
the reversion and therefore Wedd, the assignee of the
original landlord, was entitled to sue; but that he could
only sue in respect of such breaches of these covenants
as occurred after he became assignee of the reversion,
that is, between December 3rd, 1912, and September
29th, 1913, when the lease came to an end.

So, for example, in the case of the undertaking
implied by Section 1, Housing Act, 1925,[1] the rights
given to the tenant accrue to the assignee of the term
and the obligation on the landlord falls on to his
assignee.

PART 2.—THE EFFECT OF DEATH.

When a person dies, his executor or administrator
is in general bound to discharge his debts and perform the contracts and covenants entered into by him.
He is not liable personally or out of his own pocket,
but merely as representing the deceased, and out of and
to the extent of the assets of the estate, and he is liable
only if a claim is made against him at the proper time.
If the deceased was a leaseholder, whether as original
tenant or as assignee, under a lease containing repairing covenants, and the covenants have been broken
during the deceased's lifetime, the executor or administrator is liable, if the landlord makes a proper claim,

[1] See *p*. 98.

to remedy those breaches out of the assets of the estate. If, however, the landlord makes no claim until the executor or administrator has fully administered, the liability of the latter is gone.

As regards breaches of the covenant to repair arising after the death of the deceased the position is not so simple.

If the deceased was the original lessee he, and after his death his estate, is liable to the lessor in privity of contract, for all breaches of the repairing covenant, by whomsoever committed for the whole duration of the lease. As long as the executor or administrator has assets of the estate in his hands he remains liable as such representative and to the extent of such assets for any future breach of the repairing covenants which may occur, but when the executor or administrator has fully administered the estate and distributed the assets, this liability terminates. If the executor or administrator has not entered or taken possession of the premises he is never personally liable out of his own pocket.[1] But if he does so enter and take possession, he makes himself an assignee of the lease and so personally liable whether there are assets or not, for all breaches of the repairing covenant which may occur while he is such assignee. He has, however, a right as against the estate to recoup himself out of the assets (if any) for whatever he may be obliged to spend on repairs.[2]

If the deceased was not the original lessee but merely an assignee, the executor or administrator, if he does not enter, is bound to remedy, out of the assets and to the extent of the assets only, any breaches that may occur after the deceased's death, and before the executor

---

[1] *Rendall* v. *Andreæ, infra.*

[2] *Tremeere* v. *Morrison,* (1834) 4 M. & Sc. 6C3 ; *Rendall* v. *Andreæ* (1892) 61 L.J. Q.B. 630.

or administrator re-assigns the property either to the person entitled thereto or to a purchaser. Of course when the executor or administrator does so assign, by assenting to a legacy,[1] conveying to the next of kin or to a purchaser the liability of the estate (as the deceased was an assignee) ceases as regards any future breaches and the new assignee becomes liable. If, when the deceased was an assignee, the executor or administrator enters and takes possession, then he makes himself personally liable, in the same way as any other assignee, for all breaches committed while he remains such assignee. But he has a right to recoup himself out of the assets (if any).

Executors and administrators have now a statutory protection, for by an Act of 1859,[2] which was re-enacted and extended by the Trustee Act, 1925,[3] personal representatives can rid themselves of all personal liability if they (1) satisfy all existing claims, (2) set aside a sufficient sum to meet all ascertained future liabilities, (3) assign the lease to a purchaser, legatee, divisee or other person.

PART 3.—THE EFFECT OF HOLDING OVER.

When a lease expires and the tenant still remains in possession, he becomes a tenant on sufferance. But when the tenant pays or agrees to pay either the same or an increased rent, nothing more being expressed between the parties as to the terms of the new tenancy, a tenancy from year to year is created on the covenants contained in the former lease, so far as they are applic-

[1] *Austin* v. *Beddoe*, (1893], W.N. 78.

[2] 22 & 23 Vict. c. 35, s. 27.

[3] Section 26.

able to, and not inconsistent with, a yearly tenancy.[1] Such yearly tenancy will be terminable at the end of the first year by a six months' notice to quit, expiring at the end of the first year.[2]

The law does not appear to be very definite as to what covenants of the former lease would be consistent with a yearly tenancy. If the lease contain an unconditional covenant to keep the premises in repair and the premises are burnt down by accidental fire during new tenancy, the tenant will be bound to rebuild.[3] Presumably a general covenant to *keep* in repair is not inconsistent with a yearly tenancy, and would be implied on a holding over. In a case where a seven years' lease contained a proviso that, unless notice was given to determine the tenancy at the end of the seven years, it should continue as a lease from year to year upon the same covenants, it was held that the lease continued after the seven years until put an end to by notice, and that the tenant was liable under his covenants to "well and substantially repair," and "so well and substantially repaired to yield up at the end of the term."[4] Whether a covenant to *leave* in repair is consistent with a yearly tenancy was expressly left open in *Blane* v. *Francis*.[5]

The question as to whether a tenant who holds over would be liable for periodical painting, etc., if specified in the former lease,[6] has not been decided. In view of the uncertainty of the law in this connection it is

---

[1] *Dougal* v. *McCarthy*, [1893] 1 Q. B. 736.

[2] *Doe* d. *Clarke* v. *Smaridge*, (1845) 7 Q.B. 957.

[3] *Digby* v. *Atkinson*, (1815) 4 Camp. 275.

[4] *Brown* v. *Trumper*, (1858) 26 Beav. 11.

[5] (1917) 1 K.B. 252 at p. 256.

[6] As, for example, under covenant set out on p. 39

always advisable that some clear understanding as to the terms of the new yearly tenancy should be arrived at between the parties.

A holding over must be carefully distinguished from a fresh agreement by which the tenant continues in possession of the demised premises from year to year or from quarter to quarter, the terms of the old lease being expressly or impliedly incorporated in the new agreement. This distinction is of importance where the landlord has assigned the reversion for on a mere holding over the assignee has no right to sue on the express covenants contained in the old lease, whereas when there is a new agreement he may be able to do so. So, where a tenant of a house for a term under a lease by deed containing repairing covenants held over after the expiration of the term, no further document being signed, and the reversion was subsequently assigned, it was held that the assignee of the reversion was not entitled to sue the tenant for breaches of the express covenant to deliver up in repair contained in the expired lease.[1] The yearly tenancy that arose after expiration of the term was not a tenancy either under seal or in writing; hence the assignee of the reversion could not enforce any express covenant.[2]

On the other hand, in a later case,[3] where part of a house had been let to a tenant for a term of years upon the terms (*inter alia*) that the tenant would " keep and *yield up* the premises in good and tenantable repair," and at the close of the term it was arranged by correspondence that the tenant should continue to occupy

---

[1] *Blane* v. *Francis*, [1917] 1 K.B. 252.

[2] See *Ante*, p. 66.

[3] *Cole* v. *Kelly*, [1920] 2 K,B. 106.

the premises on a quarterly tenancy, the Court held, there being no new express agreement as to repairs, that the terms of the expired lease for years as to repairs were to be implied in the new agreement for a quarterly tenancy; that this agreement was in writing; and that consequently an assignee of the landlord could sue upon the covenant.[1]

---

[1] See also *Rye* v. *Purcell*, [1926] 1 K.B. 446.

CHAPTER VI.

LIABILITY ARISING FROM CONTRACT
(continued).

PART 1.— THE TENANT'S REMEDIES.

IN the case of furnished houses, as already explained in Chapter III, the tenant's remedy for breach by the landlord of the *implied condition* of the contract of tenancy that the premises are fit for habitation at the time of letting, is to repudiate the tenancy. Or, if the tenant has suffered injury owing to the breach of this implied term of the tenancy contract, he can sue the landlord for damages.[1]

When the landlord expressly agrees to repair, the tenant can sue him for breach of such agreement. The measure of damages in such cases has already been dealt with.[2]

PART 2.—THE LANDLORD'S REMEDIES.

The remedies open to the landlord are three:—

1. He may bring an action for damages.

2. He may enter the premises and carry out the necessary repairs and sue the tenant for the cost. This remedy, however, is only possible when a right to enter and repair has been expressly reserved in the lease.

3. He may re-enter upon the premises and obtain forfeiture of the lease. This remedy is only possible if the lease provides for forfeiture for breach of the covenant to repair, and is subject to certain statutory provisions.

---

[1] *Charsley* v. *Jones*, (1889) 5 T.L.R. 412.

[2] See *ante*, p. 31.

An injunction to compel either a tenant or a landlord to put or keep premises in repair will never be granted.

1. An action for damages for breach of an express contract to repair may be brought at any time during the lease, or after the lease has expired. If the lease is under seal, the action will be on the covenant to repair and may be brought at any time within twenty years after the breach; where the lease is not under seal, the action must, under the Statutes of Limitation, be brought within six years. This distinction is of little importance, since in practice the action is usually brought soon after the breach.

An action can also be brought against the tenant for breach of the *implied* contract to keep in repair referred to in Chapter III., but as there pointed out this seldom arises in practice, since nearly all leases contain an express contract to repair.

If during a lease the landlord considers that repairs are necessary, or if the lease is about to terminate, shortly before such termination, he usually gives the tenant notice that he or his surveyor intends to go over the property on a certain date in order to examine the state of repair and to see whether the covenants contained in the lease have been carried out. The landlord can only enter and view the state of repair if a proviso entitling him to do so has been inserted in the lease, and practically every lease or agreement contains such a proviso. In the absence of such a provision the landlord is liable to an action for trespass if he enter the premises for this purpose.

When a lease is coming to an end, and particularly in cases where the landlord is making a claim for damages, the tenant often appoints a surveyor to meet the landlord's surveyor and go over the premises with him and agree (if possible) as to the extent of the tenant's liability for defects or necessary repairs due to the failure of the tenant to fulfil his obligation under his repairing covenant. Or, the landlord and tenant may agree to abide by the report and valuation of the cost of repairs, to be made by a surveyor mutually agreed upon, in which case both will be bound by such valuation. More often, perhaps, the schedule of repairs is prepared by the landlord's surveyor and also an estimate of their cost, which amount is claimed from the tenant, who, if he considers it unreasonable, appoints another surveyor to investigate the claim on his behalf. In many cases a settlement is arrived at between the two surveyors, or, as is very often done, the points in dispute are referred to the decision of a third surveyor acting as arbitrator. If, however, no settlement is effected, the landlord commences an action to recover damages for breach of the agreement to repair, and the matter is decided by the Courts. If the amount claimed does not exceed £100, the action can be tried in the County Court; if over that amount, in the High Court, unless the parties consent to the jurisdiction of the County Court. Or the parties can agree to settle the dispute by arbitration. When an action of this kind is brought in the High Court it is usual for the Court to refer it to an Official Referee (a permanent officer of the Court) to assess the damage, or to a Special Referee (generally an architect or surveyor appointed for that purpose by the Court). If the action is brought in the County Court it can only be referred to a referee by consent of both parties.

The measure of damages for breach of a repairing covenant or agreement differs according to whether the action is brought while the lease is still running on a covenant or agreement to keep in repair, or at the end of lease on a covenant or agreement to keep, put or leave in repair.

(a) If the lease is still running, the action is brought on the contract or covenant *to keep the premises in repair*. It is impossible to lay down any hard and fast rule as to what damages may be recovered by the landlord, as all the circumstances of each case must be taken into consideration. The damage should be such as reasonably represents the damage which the landlord has sustained by the breach of covenant, or, in other words, the amount by which his reversion is depreciated in market value. Obviously this amount will vary according to the length of time the lease has still to run. For instance, in the case of a 99 years' lease with 96 years still unexpired, the tenant's neglect to repair, would, at that date, make very little difference to the marketable value of the reversion, and the amount of damages recoverable would be very small; whereas supposing, in the same case, 96 years had expired and the property was going to revert to the landlord in three years' time, then the neglect of the tenant to repair might cause serious injury to the value of the landlord's reversion, and the amount of damages would be almost as much as the actual cost of the necessary repairs. In order to arrive at the depreciation in value of the reversion, it is necessary to determine " the difference in value between the reversion with the covenant performed as it ought to be and the value of that reversion with the covenant unperformed, which it ought not to be."[1]

The landlord is under no obligation to devote the sum which he recovers by way of damages to carrying

[1] Per Lindley, L.J., in *Ebbetts* v. *Conquest*, [1895] 2 Ch. 377, p. 383 ; affirmed by House of Lords, [1896] A.C. 490.

out repairs to the premises. Moreover, the injury is a continuing one, which means that the landlord can sue for damages once, and then sue again later if the covenant is still being broken.

(b) If the lease has come to an end, the action is brought on either the covenant to keep in repair, or the covenant to deliver up in repair. Before 26th March, 1928, when an action was brought at the end of a lease, on the contract to yield up, or to leave, in repair, the measure of damages which the landlord could recover was the reasonable and proper amount necessary to put the premises into the state of repair in which they ought to have been left in accordance with the repairing covenant,[1] regard being had to the class of property and its age. In addition to this, the landlord was entitled to compensation for the loss of the use of the premises while they were under repair, but this compensation was not necessarily the full rent of the premises during the time.[2]

Even if the landlord pulled down the building after the termination of the lease, the tenant's liability was unaffected,[3] and this was also the case if, during the lease, the landlord had granted to a new tenant a lease, to commence immediately after the expiration of the former one, wherein the new tenant covenanted to pull down and alter part of the premises and keep them in repair. The contract between the landlord and a third person could not be taken into account, and did not in any way affect the obligations of the tenant under his repairing covenant.[4]

---

[1] *Joyner* v. *Weeks*, [1891] 2 Q.B. 31.

[2] *Woods* v. *Pope*, (1835) 6 C. & P. 782; *Birch* v. *Clifford*, (1891) 8 T.L.R. 103.

[3] *Inderwick* v. *Leech*, (1884) 1 T.L.R. 95, 484.

[4] *Joyner* v. *Weeks, supra.*

This rule of law was an inequitable one, for it sometimes involved a large sum being paid by the tenant for repairs which the landlord never intended to execute. The difficulty, however, was (and still is) this—that but for the rule, a tenant who has broken his contract might be in a better position than a tenant who has kept it, a result which the Courts would not encourage.

The law in this respect has been altered by Section 18 (1) of the Landlord and Tenant Act, 1927, which came into operation on 25th March, 1928. This section, which applies to leases whether created before or after the commencement of the Act,[1] provides that, " Damages for the breach of a covenant or agreement to keep or put premises in repair during the currency of a lease, or to leave or put premises in repair at the termination of a lease whether such covenant or agreement is expressed or implied, and whether general or specific, shall in no case exceed the amount (if any), by which the value of the reversion (whether immediate or not) in the premises is diminished owing to the breach . . . . ; and, in particular no damage shall be recovered for a breach of any such covenant or agreement to leave or put premises in repair at the termination of a lease, if it is shown that the premises, in whatever state of repair they might be, would at or shortly after the termination of the tenancy have been or be pulled down, or such structural alterations made therein as would render valueless the repairs covered by the covenant or agreement."

Whether the section has any effect on the principle in Calthorpe's case,[2] and, if so, what that effect is, are questions which will have to be settled by the Courts.

[1] See Sect. 18 (3).

[2] See *supra*. p. 54, *et seq.*

The above remarks apply to the relationship of land-lord and tenant. The position as between a lessee and an under-lessee requires separate consideration. Suppose, for example A leases premises to B for a term of years, and B subleases to C for the remainder of the term less three days; and suppose both the lease and sub-lease contain a repairing covenant in the same or similar terms. If C fails to repair, B has a right of action. But the measure of damages is obviously not the loss in value of B's reversion for the value of B's reversion is negligible. In such cases the liability of the lessee to the lessor must be taken into account in assessing the liability of the under-lessee to the lessee. Thus in the case of *Ebbetts* v. *Conquest and Booth*,[1] the plaintiffs were trustees, under the Will of a deceased tenant, of certain premises held for a term of 61 years from 1837. An under-lease for the whole term (less ten days) had been granted to one of the defendants, the other defendant being the assignee of the under-lease. Both the lease and the under-lease contained substantially the same repairing covenants, and this action was brought by the plaintiffs to recover damages for breach of the covenant to keep in repair. It was not denied that there had been a breach, and by order of the Court the matter was referred to the Official Referee to assess the amount of damages. Evidence was given to show that at the end of the term, the site would have to be cleared, the only profitable way of dealing with it being to treat it as a build-ing site. The evidence went to show that if the buildings were put into repair they would be worth £200 more to pull down and carry away than if not put into repair. The defendants contended, therefore, that at most the value of the plaintiffs' (the under-lessors) re-

---

[1] (1895) 2 Ch. 377.

version had only been diminished to the extent of £200 by the want of repair. The Official Referee did not adopt this view, but held that, as the plaintiffs at the expiration of their lease would, under the covenants of the original lease, have to pay the full expense of putting the buildings into proper repair, that expense must be taken into account in assessing the damage they had sustained. He therefore assessed the damage on the principle that in an action brought before the term has expired for a breach of covenant to keep in repair, you must look at the value of the under-lessors' reversion. In this case the term was very nearly at an end—it had three and a half to four years to run. The value of the ten days' reversion (reserved in the under-lease), if the property had been in repair, would be so much; if the property had been out of repair it would be so much; and the difference amounted to £1,305. He arrived at that result in this way. He held that the expense of putting the buildings in repair would be £1,500; but allowing a discount for the time to elapse before that sum would become payable, he obtained the above result of £1,305. This decision was appealed against, but the principle adopted by the Official Referee was upheld by the Court of Appeal and subsequently by the House of Lords.

It should be noted that in this case it was known to the under-tenant that his immediate landlord (the original tenant) was liable to yield up the premises in repair, and therefore (being known to and reasonably within the contemplation of the under-tenant) this liability was one of the circumstances to be considered in the assessment of damages. It should also be noted that had this case been heard to-day, it would have been decided differently. Section 18 of the Landlord and Tenant Act, 1927, applies to under-leases as well as leases.[1] As the site was to be cleared, the lessor would be able to recover nothing under his repairing covenant. Consequently, in assessing damages against the under-lessee, nothing would have had to be brought into account in respect of the lessee's liability under the head lease.

Moreover, the lessee cannot always recover from the under-lessee the whole of the amount for which he is liable to the lessor, even where the covenants in the lease and under-lease are identical, for the lease and the under-lease may be (and generally are) entered into at different times and cover different periods. And when an action on the covenant has been brought by the lessor against the lessee, the latter cannot recover the costs he has incurred as damages in an action against the under-lessee.

In a case[2] where a landlord gave notice to his immediate tenant to repair, at the peril of forfeiting his lease for breach of covenant, the tenant, who had under-let part of the premises, thereupon gave his under-tenant a similar notice to repair within three months. The under-tenant, however, neglected to do so, whereupon the original tenant, in order to prevent a forfeiture of his whole estate entered and put the premises in tenantable repair. It was held that though he might be a trespasser for so doing, yet he might recover from his under-tenant the whole expense incurred, although the latter had sold his interest in the premises to a purchaser, who had entirely rebuilt them before the action for the recovery of such expense was brought.

In another similar case,[3] the tenants were under a general covenant required to repair, and also under a

---

[1] See definition of "Lease" in Section 25 (1).

[2] *Colley* v. *Streeton*, (1823) 2 B. & C. 273.

[3] *Williams* v. *Williams*, (1874) L.R., 9 C.P. 659 ; 43 L.J., C.P. 382.

covenant to repair within three months of notice to do so, and they had sub-let, the under-lease containing similar covenants by the under-tenant to repair, except that the notice stipulated for was a two months' notice. Notice was given to the under-tenant, but before the expiration of the *two* months the tenants, in order to avoid a forfeiture, entered and did the repairs themselves, and then, also before the expiration of the *two* months, sued the under-tenant for breach of covenant. The Court held that they could only recover nominal damages on the general covenant, since by having done the necessary repairs they had, at the time the action was brought, sustained no injury to their reversion;[1] and that they could recover nothing on the special covenant, the action having been brought too soon.

In an action[2] for damages for breach of covenant to repair contained in an under-lease, owing to which it was alleged that the under-lessors' term had been forfeited, it was held that the latter could not recover from the under-tenants damages for the loss of their term, since the superior landlord had brought his action for ejectment not only on the ground of breach of the covenant to repair, but also for breach of another covenant not contained in the under-lease.

2. Apart from an express stipulation in the lease, and from the right given him under certain Acts of Parliament, the landlord has no right to enter his tenant's premises, either to view the state of repair or to effect the repairs. A landlord who, in the absence

---

[1] It seems difficult to reconcile this case (*Williams* v. *Williams*) with the case (*Colley* v. *Streeton*) last referred to, and it may be doubted whether *Williams* v. *Williams* is still good law on the first point involved, in the view of the principles enunciated in *Ebbetts* v. *Conquest* (*supra*).

[2] *Clow* v. *Brogden*, (1840) 2 M. & G. 39.

of such stipulation, enters upon the demised premises to repair them on breach of the tenant's covenant to repair, commits a trespass which will be restrained by injunction,[1] notwithstanding that under a superior lease the landlord is liable to forfeiture for non-repair, and notwithstanding that he enters by leave of weekly sub-tenants.

When, however, the right is reserved, the landlord may enter and repair, and recover from the tenant, by action, the cost of repairs which the tenant was liable to execute under his repairing covenant. This is so at all events when the lease or agreement contains an express provision that the landlord shall be entitled to recover such cost from the tenant, and a provision to this effect is usually inserted. When it is not inserted it may be argued that the landlord ought not to be able merely by virtue of a stipulation giving him the right to enter and do the repairs, to recover the whole cost thereof when, in the absence of such a stipulation, he might be able to recover only a nominal sum representing the loss to the reversion.

3. Most leases contain a proviso that, in the event of breach or non-observance by the tenant of any of the covenants and agreements contained therein, it shall be lawful for the landlord to re-enter and take possession of the premises. Formerly, when such a proviso existed and a breach of covenant occurred, the landlord (or his assigns) might at once re-enter, or if the tenant refused peaceably to admit him, the landlord might bring what is now technically known as " an action for the recovery of land," formerly, and still popularly, called " an action of ejectment."

---

[1] *Stocker* v. *Planet Building Society*, (1879) 27 W.R. 877.

This, however, was in many cases a great hardship on the tenant, and now, by the Law of Property Act,[1] 1925, s. 146, the landlord's right of forfeiture for breach of covenant (other than the covenant to pay rent, and others specified in sub-sections 6 and 8) is not enforceable either by peaceable re-entry or by bringing an action[2] until the landlord has served on the tenant a written notice specifying the particular breach complained of, and if the breach is capable of remedy, requiring the lessee to remedy the breach, and, in any case, requiring the tenant to make compensation in money for such breach; and the tenant has failed to remedy the breach and make reasonable compensation within a reasonable time. A " reasonable time " is, in practice, generally taken to be three months. Under the same section the Court may, on the application of the tenant, grant relief against forfeiture on such terms as it thinks fit.

The section is as follows :—

(1).—A right of re-entry or forfeiture under any proviso or stipulation in a lease, for a breach of any covenant or condition in the lease, shall not be enforceable, by action or otherwise, unless and until the lessor serves on the lessee a notice specifying the particular breach complained of and, if the breach is capable of remedy, requiring the lessee to remedy the breach, and in any case requiring the lessee to make compensation in money for the breach, and the lessee fails, within a reasonable time thereafter, to remedy the breach, if it is capable of remedy, and to make reasonable compensation in money, to the satisfaction of the lessor, for the breach.

(2).—Where the lessor is proceeding, by action or otherwise, to enforce such a right of re-entry or forfeiture, the lessee may, in the lessor's action, if any, or in any action brought by himself, apply to the Court for relief; and the Court may grant or refuse relief, as the Court, having regard to the proceedings and conduct of the parties under the foregoing provisions of

---

[1] Re-enacting Conveyancing Act, 1881, s. 14.

[2] *Riggs, In re* ; *Ex parte Lovell*, [1901] 2 K.B, 16.

this section, and to all the other circumstances, thinks fit; and in case of relief may grant it on such terms, if any, as to costs, expenses, damages, compensation, penalty or otherwise, including the granting of an injunction to restrain any like breach in the future, as the Court, in the circumstances of each case thinks fit.

The position, therefore, is that the landlord cannot recover possession by action or otherwise until the provisions of sub-section 1 are satisfied. Even when they are satisfied, the tenant may still obtain relief against forfeiture from the Court under sub-section 2, if the Court thinks fit to grant it. The Court will generally grant relief if the tenant makes compensation or undertakes to remedy the breach. Relief may be asked for by the tenant by way of counterclaim in an action brought by the lessor, or in a separate action brought by himself.

The grant of relief is discretionary. " It seems to me," said Earl Loreburn, L.C., " that when the Act is so express to provide a wide discretion, meaning, no doubt, to prevent one man from forfeiting what in fair dealing belongs to someone else, by taking advantage of a breach from which he is not commensurately and irreparably damaged, it is not advisable to lay down any rigid rules for guiding that discretion.[1]

The law with regard to the service of notice has in the case of covenants to put or keep or leave in repair been modified by the Landlord and Tenant Act, 1927, s. 18 (2). Previously service of notice was necessary and sufficient, and service could be effected by leaving the notice at the last-known place of abode or business of the lessee or by sending it by registered post to such last-known address. By the above section the lessor must prove not only the fact of service but also knowledge of that fact on the part of the lessee, or of an

---

[1] *Hyman* v. *Rose*. [1912] A.C. at p. 631.

under-lessee holding the premises by virtue of an
under-lease which reserves only a nominal reversion to
the lessee (*e.g.*, where A leases to B for seven years
and B under-leases to C for seven years less three
days), or of the person who last paid the rent due
under the lease either on his own behalf or as agent
for the lessee or under-lessee. Where notice is served
by registered post, knowledge of service is presumed
unless the contrary be proved.

The notice must be given in such detail as will
enable the tenant to understand what is complained of,
so that he may have an opportunity of remedying the
breach before action is brought. A mere general
notice of breach of a specified covenant is not sufficient. For instance, where a notice by the landlord to
the tenant was as follows:—" You have broken the
covenants for repairing the inside and outside of the
houses, Nos. 10, 11, 12, etc., Blank Street, contained
in a lease of the said premises, dated, etc." and claiming £20 compensation, an action to recover possession
and also damages for breach of covenant was dismissed, on the ground that notice " specifying the
particular breach of covenant complained of " had not
been given.[1] In a later case it was for the same reason
held that a notice to the tenant " that you have not
kept the said premises well and sufficiently repaired
and the party and other walls thereof," was insufficient. The fact that such a notice sufficiently speci-
fies other breaches of covenant which are complained
of will not make the notice sufficient.[2]

But a notice referring to several distinct alleged
breaches of covenant is not altogether invalidated

---

[1] *Fletcher* v. *Nokes*, [1897] 1 Ch. 271.
[2] *Serle. In re: Gregory* v. *Serle*, [1898] 1 Ch. 652.

because it transpires that, although some of the alleged breaches have occurred, the others have never taken place, or that the landlord is not entitled to rely on them.[1]

The question of the sufficiency of a notice has now received the consideration of the House of Lords in *Fox* v. *Jolly*.[2] The notice was served by the lessor of six small houses stating that the repairing covenants as set out therein had been broken, and that the particular breaches complained of were the committing or allowing the dilapidations mentioned in the schedule annexed to the notice. The schedule indicated, under general headings, repairs which were required to be done in all the houses, and in a few instances only specified repairs to be done in particular houses. In some instances it required the lessee " to examine and repair " specified parts of the houses. The schedule concluded with the words " And note that the completion of the items mentioned in this schedule does not excuse the execution of other repairs if found necessary." It was held that the notice sufficiently specified the particular breaches complained of, and that it was not vitiated by the addition of the general clause at the end.

A notice under this section requiring the tenant to remedy a breach of covenant will be good even if it does not require payment of compensation in money.[3]

From the foregoing it will be apparent that the notice of breach of covenant to repair should always be followed by a schedule of the required repairs.

---

[1] *Pannell* v. *City of London Brewery Co.*, [1900] 1 Ch. 496.

[2] [1916] 1 A.C. 1 affirming *Jolly* v. *Brown*, [1914] 2 K.B., 109.

[3] *Lock* v. *Pearce*, [1893] 2 Ch. 271.

The form of Notice is generally in the following terms :—

To *John Jones* and all parties interested.

I HEREBY GIVE YOU NOTICE that you have committed breaches of the covenant to repair the house, *No.* 10, *Blank Street,* which you hold of me under a lease dated the *5th day of April,* 1904, containing such covenant. The particulars of the said breaches are specified in the Schedule hereto.

AND I hereby require you, within *three* calendar months from the date of this Notice, to remedy the said breaches [and to pay me the sum of £20 as compensation for the same].

(Signed) *RICHARD SMITH.*

Dated this 11*th day of August,* 1924.

The Schedule above referred to.

A proviso in a lease, giving the landlord a right to re-enter for breach of covenant, does not deprive him of his right to bring an action for damages for breach of covenant.

Where the breach of covenant is not a continuing one, a right of re-entry is waived by the landlord bringing an action for or accepting rent accruing subsequently to the breach, with a knowledge of its existence,[1] as, for instance, after a breach of a covenant to *put* premises into repair forthwith.

The breach of a covenant " to *keep* in repair " is a continuing breach, *i.e.,* one which goes on and is added to from day to day; as opposed to a breach committed by one definite act on the part of the tenant. Under a covenant " to keep in repair," a tenant must have the premises in repair at all times during the term, and if at any time they are out of repair he is guilty of a breach of covenant, for which, if the lease so provides, the landlord can, after due notice, claim forfeiture, or he may bring an action for damages, either during the continuance or after the termination of the lease.

---

[1] *Dendy* v. *Nicholl*, (1858) 4 C.B. (N.S.) 376.

In one instance a lease contained a general covenant
to keep in repair and a covenant to repair within three
months after notice, and the premises being out of
repair, the landlord gave the tenant notice under Section 14 of the Conveyancing Act, 1881,[1] to repair within
three months. Three days before the expiration of the
notice a quarter's rent became due. The tenant failed
to comply with the notice, and the landlord brought an
action to recover possession, the quarter's rent, and
damages for breach of covenant. The Court held that
as the breach of covenant was a continuing one, no new
notice was required in respect of the non-repair after
the expiration of the time specified in the notice, and
that the claim for rent did not affect the right to
possession in respect of non-repair after the date when
the rent became due.[2]

In a more recent case the landlord accepted from the
tenant a half-year's rent which had accrued due since
the date when the notice, served in pursuance of Section 14, had expired. In an action to recover possession of the premises in respect of the continuing breach
of covenant arising out of the non-repair since the date
when the rent so accepted became due, it was held
that, as the only object of the notice was to inform
the tenant what she was required to do, no new notice
was necessary to support the action, even though so
long an interval as twelve months had elapsed between
the date of the expiry of the notice and the commencement of the action, and though the tenant had done a
portion of the required repairs in that period, so that
the physical condition of the premises which the tenant
was required to make good was not the same when the

---

[1] Which is now re-enacted by the above provisions of the Law of
Property Act.

[2] *Penton* v. *Barnett*, [1898] 1 Q.B. 276.

action was brought as when the notice was given. The tenant knew what he had been required to do, and what he had left undone, and that was sufficient to keep the notice applicable.[1]

A covenant to erect certain buildings within a definite time is not a continuing covenant, even though it is followed by a covenant to keep the premises "so to be erected as aforesaid in good and substantial repair "; and in such a case no further covenant to build can be implied from the covenant to repair.[2]

Although the acceptance of rent after service of a notice to repair would not act as a waiver of a subsequent right of re-entry arising from non-compliance with such notice, yet in receiving rent from a tenant upon whom such a notice has been served, it is a good practice to give the receipt " without prejudice to the notice to repair."

So much for the position as between landlord and tenant. These provisions did not afford any protection to an under-tenant, so if A leased to B, and B underleased to C, C's interest was liable to forfeiture on breach of a covenant in A's lease to B, although C had himself observed all the covenants in the under-lease from B to himself. This position was dealt with by Section 4 of the Conveyancing and Law of Property Act, 1892,[3] which provides that where a landlord is proceeding to enforce a forfeiture the Court may, on the application of the under-lessee of the whole or any part of the property comprised in the lease, either in the landlord's action (if any), or in any action brought by the under-lessee for that purpose, make an order vesting for the whole term of the lease, or any less

---

[1] *New River Co.* v. *Crumpton*, [1917] 1 K.B. 762.

[2] *Jacob* v. *Down*, [1900] 2 Ch. 156 and *Stephens* v. *Junior Army and Navy Stores*, [1914] 2 Ch. 516.

[3] Re-enacted by Law of Property Act, 1925, s. 146 (4).

term, the property comprised in the lease, or any part thereof, in any such under-lessee, upon such conditions as to execution of any deed or other document, payment of rent, costs, expenses, damages, compensation, giving security, or otherwise, as the Court in the circumstances of each case shall think fit; but in no case shall the under-lessee be entitled to require a lease to be granted to him for any longer term than he had under his original under-lease.

Where a lease has been forfeited for breaches by a lessee of a covenant to repair, the fact that an under-lessee has broken a similar covenant contained in the under-lease does not prevent the latter from obtaining relief under Section 4 of the Conveyancing Act, 1892.[1]

The lessor is not entitled to recover from his tenant the expenses incurred in employing a surveyor to prepare a schedule of repairs unless :—

(i) The tenant has expressly agreed in the lease or agreement to pay such expenses; or

(ii) The landlord has the right to recover such expenses by virtue of the Law of Property Act, 1925, Section 146 (3).

This sub-section[2] is as follows :—

" A lessor shall be entitled to recover as a debt due to him from a lessee, and in addition to damages (if any) all reasonable costs and expenses properly incurred by the lessor in the employment of a solicitor and surveyor or valuer, or otherwise, in reference to any breach giving rise to a right of re-entry or forfeiture which, at the request of the lessee, is waived by the lessor by writing under his hand, or from which the lessee is relieved, under the provisions of this Act."

An under-tenant (even of the whole of the premises included in the head-lease) is a " lessee " within the

---

[1] *Hurd* v. *Whaley*, [1918] 1 K.B. 448.

[2] Re-enacting Section 2 (1) of the Conveyancing Act (1881).

meaning of this sub-section,[1] and therefore the landlord can recover from him the costs of a solicitor and surveyor incurred in preparing a Schedule of Repairs.

In a case where the landlord sought to recover such expenses incurred in respect of the preparation of a notice of breach of covenant, required by Section 14 (1) of the Conveyancing and Law of Property Act, 1881, as " compensation " for which the tenant is liable in lieu of forfeiture, the Court of Appeal held that such expenses arose " not from the breach of the covenant, but solely from the fetter which the wisdom of the Legislature has imposed on the enforcement of the cause of action arising from that breach,"[2] and the tenant was, therefore, not liable for them.

---

[1] See Sect. 146 (5) *Nind* v. *Nineteenth Century Building Society*, (1894) 2 Q.B. 226, which was decided under the corresponding Section of the Conveyancing Act, (1881) must be taken to be overruled.

[2] Per Fry, L.J. *Skinners' Company* v. *Knight*, [1891] 2 Q.B., at page 545.

CHAPTER VII.

LIABILITY ARISING BY STATUTE.

PART 1.—GENERAL.

PARLIAMENT has not left the repair of buildings, and the incidence of the liability for such repair to be governed entirely by agreement, but has interfered in several ways, sometimes by imposing liability where otherwise no liability would exist, and sometimes by making it impossible for a landlord by agreement to saddle his tenant with repairing obligations.

An exhaustive analysis of the various Acts relating to dilapidations is impossible, because they have not been based on any well-defined principles, but have been passed to serve particular social or political ends. The provisions of these Acts may, however, be grouped under three heads :—

1. Provisions designed to relieve poverty.
2. Provisions designed to promote public health.
3. Provisions designed to secure public safety.

Before dealing with these three heads in turn, the provisions of an Act relating to damage caused by fire must be examined. The liability of a tenant for damage caused by fire is partly governed by the terms of the lease or tenancy agreement, and ought therefore to have been treated in the foregoing chapter. But, inasmuch as it is also governed by statute, the whole subject has been postponed for consideration here.

PART 2.—PROVISION RELATING TO DAMAGE CAUSED BY FIRE.

Unless there is an express covenant to repair a landlord cannot sue his tenant for damages arising from accidental fire; but if there is a general covenant by the tenant to repair the premises, and no exception is made for damage by fire, the tenant must rebuild them if they are burnt down by accident, negligence, or otherwise.[1] Further, unless the lease provides to the contrary, the tenant will continue liable to pay rent until the end of his lease, even though the premises are uninhabitable.[2]

The tenant who has agreed to repair, in a lease containing no proviso that damage by fire is excepted, should, therefore, himself insure the premises against damage by fire, and by paying an increased premium he can also insure against payment of rent during the reinstatement of the building, or while it is untenantable in consequence of fire, and against architects' and surveyors' fees necessarily incurred in the restoration of the building.

The freedom of the tenant from liability for accidental fire when there is no express covenant to repair arises by Statute. Section 86 of the Fires Prevention (Metropolis) Act, 1774,[3] (this section, together with Section 83, being the only ones now in force, the remainder of the Act having been repealed) provides that " no action, suit or process whatever shall be had, maintained, or prosecuted against any person in whose house, chamber, stable or other building, or on whose estate any fire shall *accidentally begin,* nor shall any recompense be made by such person for any damage suffered thereby . . . . provided that no contract or agreement made between landlord and tenant shall be hereby defeated or made void." In other words, the Act does not affect an express covenant to repair.[4]

---

[1] *Bullock* v. *Dommitt*, (1796) 6 T.R, 650.

[2] *Baker* v. *Holtpzaffell*, (1811) 4 Taunt. 45.

[3] 14 Geo. III., c. 78.

[4] See Note on this Statute in Appendix.

The Statute, which is not limited to the Metropolis but has been held to apply to the whole kingdom, must be taken only to refer to fires which are the result of chance, or which are incapable of being traced to any cause, and not to fires which, although they may be accidental as opposed to wilful, are occasioned by negligence or want of reasonable care.

Usually in three years' agreements and in shorter tenancies there is a proviso inserted in the repairing clause, " Damage by fire excepted," and when this is so, the tenant will not be liable to rebuild in case of fire, but it should be remembered that the release of the tenant from liability does not impose on the landlord any obligation to rebuild after fire, neither does it relieve the tenant from his liability to pay rent. In some leases the landlord undertakes to insure the premises and to expend the insurance money in rebuilding, and also relinquishes his right to rent while the premises are uninhabitable. When this is so, the covenants are generally to the following effect. The landlord covenants :—

" To keep the demised premises insured against loss or damage by fire and in the case of damage or destruction by fire (unless the insurance money become irrecoverable through any act or default of the tenant) to rebuild and reinstate the same as speedily as possible.

" In case the demised premises or any part thereof shall at any time during the said term be destroyed or damaged by fire so as to be unfit for occupation and use, and the policy or policies effected by the landlord shall not have been vitiated or payment of the policy moneys refused in consequence of some act or default of the tenant the rent hereby reserved or a fair proportion thereof according to the nature and extent of the damage sustained shall cease and be suspended until the said premises shall be again rendered fit for occupation and use and in the case of difference touching this proviso the same shall be referred to arbitration."

In longer leases the tenant generally covenants to insure the premises for a specified sum against fire. If he also covenants to repair, his liability will not be limited to the amount received from the Insurance Company, but he will have to pay, out of his own pocket, whatever balance is necessary to reinstate the premises in their former condition,[1] and, as already stated, he will have to continue paying rent until the end of the term.

If a tenant has unconditionally agreed to repair, he will have to rebuild after fire, even if the landlord has insured and has received the insurance money[2] as the latter is only bound to rebuild when he has expressly covenanted to do so.

A policy of fire insurance is, however, a contract of indemnity (*i.e.*, one to make good another's loss caused by some specific act) ; and if the landlord has insured a house and received the insurance money, but the tenant has, under his repairing covenant, rebuilt the premises, the Insurance Company can recover from the landlord the money which they have paid him on his policy.

Provision has also been made by Section 83 of the Fires Prevention (Metropolis) Act, 1774,[3] for ensuring that money due under a fire policy is expended in re-building.

The effect of the section is as follows :—When a house or building which is insured has been damaged by fire, the directors of the Insurance Company shall, *if requested by any person or persons interested in or entitled unto* such houses or other buildings (the expression " person interested " seems to include the

---

[1] *Digby* v. *Atkinson.* (1815) 4 Camp. 275.

[2] *Leeds* v. *Cheetham*, (1827) 1 Sim. 146.

[3] See whole section in Appendix.

tenant as well as the landlord) cause the insurance money to be expended, in so far as it will go, in rebuilding the premises, unless the person claiming the insurance money shall within sixty days after his claim is adjusted, give a sufficient security to the directors that the money will be laid out in rebuilding. The directors have similar power, without any request being made to them, if they have any grounds for suspicion that the person who has insured has been guilty of fraud or has wilfully set the building on fire.

In order to entitle the landlord to the benefit of this section he must make a distinct request to the Insurance Company to lay out the insurance money in rebuilding before they have settled with the tenant insuring; and in no case is the landlord entitled to rebuild the premises himself, and then claim the insurance money.[1]

Trade fixtures put up by a tenant and removable by him do not come within the words " houses or other buildings."[2]

This section has been held to apply not only to London but to the whole of the Kingdom,[3] although an opinion has been expressed in the House of Lords that it does not apply to Scotland.[4]

If the landlord has insured and the tenant has not, and the demised premises are burnt down, the tenant should at once request the Insurance Company to lay out the policy money in rebuilding. If, however, the landlord is under covenant to rebuild in case of fire, this will not be necessary, as the landlord will be bound by his covenant.

---

[1] *Simpson* v. *Scottish Union Insurance Co.*, (1863) 1 H. & M. 618.

[2] *Gorely, Ex. parte ; In re Barker*, (1864) 34 L.J.B.K. 1.

[3] *Ibid.*

[4] *Westminster Fire Office*, v. *Glasgow Provident Investment Society*, (1888) 13 App, Cas. 699; per Earl of Selborne and Lord Watson, at p. 716.

If, in pursuance of an express covenant, the tenant
has insured the building, it is seldom that any question
arises, for if the lease expressly provides for insuring, it
invariably also provides for rebuilding, and of course
in most cases it is to the tenant's interest to rebuild as
soon as possible.

A tenant who, after the expiration of a lease, " holds
over " and pays rent, will be liable to rebuild the premises if they are burnt down, if the former lease contained a covenant to keep the premises in repair, with
no exception for damage by fire.[1]

PART 3.—PROVISIONS DESIGNED TO RELIEVE POVERTY.

By the Housing Act, 1925, Section 1, if a house or
part of a house is let at a rent which does not exceed
£40 a year within the Administrative County of London or £26 a year elsewhere in England, Wales and
Scotland, there is an *implied condition by the landlord* (except where the house has been let for a term
of at least three years certain, upon the terms that
the tenant will put the house into a condition reasonably fit for occupation and the lease is not determinable
at the option of either party before the expiration
of that term), *that the house is, in all respects,
reasonably fit for human habitation,* and *an implied
undertaking* that the landlord *will keep it in that state*
during the whole of the tenancy. These conditions are
implied notwithstanding any provisions to the contrary
contained in the tenancy agreement. Consequently
a landlord cannot by express agreement with the tenant
rid himself of his liability under this section.

The tenant of such a house has a remedy by action
against the landlord on these implied covenants for

---

[1] *Digby* v. *Atkinson*, (1815) 4 Camp. 275.

any damage he may have suffered as a result of their breach.   In a case[1] tried before Mr. Justice Scrutton and a jury, the tenant sued his landlord and recovered £50 damages for personal injuries sustained through a breach of the implied contract under the above Act. While the tenant was sitting outside an upstairs window of his house, and cleaning the glass, the sash gave way, and he fell, sustaining severe injuries.   In another case[2] under the Act, a tenant received £5 5s. damages from his landlord owing to the house being infested with bugs.   In a later case,[3] however, where rats did not live or breed in the house, but habitually came into the house from a near-by sewer, it was held that there was no breach of the condition that *the house* should be fit for human habitation.   It must be noted, however, that it is only the tenant who can sue, and it is only for damages caused to him that the landlord will be liable.   So, where the tenant's wife suffered injury owing to the premises being out of repair, it was held that she had no cause of action against the landlord.[4] In addition to his remedy in damages, the tenant may quit the house without paying rent if either of these implied conditions is broken.

The general rule[5] that a tenant cannot recover damages unless the landlord had notice of the defect applies to cases under the statutory covenant as well as to those under express covenants.   In *Fisher* v. *Walters*[6] it was held that, where the tenant was pre-

---

[1] *Schnell* v. *Chamberlain*, [1911] unreported.

[2] *Smith* v. *Herbert*, reported in *The Times* 26th July, 1911, p. 15.

[3] *Stanton* v. *Southwick*, [1920] 2 K.B. 642.

[4] *Middleton* v. *Hall*, (1913) 108 L.T. 804 ; *Ryall* v. *Kidwell*. [1913] 3 K.B. 123.

[5] See p. 29.

[6] (1926) 2 K.B. 315.

cluded from giving such notice because, owing to the
latent nature of the defect, he did not know of its
existence, and could not by exercising ordinary care
have found out, he might recover damages. On the
other hand, in *Morgan* v. *Liverpool Corporation*[1] a
window of a house let by the defendants to the plaintiff,
owing to a defective cord, slipped down and injured
the plaintiff's hand. Two of the Judges of the Court
of Appeal were of opinion that such a defect did not
render a house not reasonably fit for human habitation.
The other Judge inclined to the view that it did. All,
however, held that the plaintiff's claim failed because
the landlord had had no notice of the defect. The
opinion was expressed that the rule applies to latent
as well as to patent defects; and this, it is submitted
must be accepted as the correct view. *Fisher* v.
Walters (supra) does not appear to have been discussed.

By Section 2 of the Act the above provisions of Section 1 are made applicable to houses occupied by workmen employed in agriculture, when the provision of a
house forms part of the remuneration of the workman,
but where there is no "letting" of the house to him.

---

[1] (1927) 2 K.B. 131.

CHAPTER VIII.

LIABILITY ARISING BY STATUTE (continued).

PART 1.—PROVISIONS DESIGNED TO PROMOTE PUBLIC HEALTH.

By Section 36 of the Public Health Act, 1875, if a house appears by the report of their Surveyor or Inspector of Nuisances to be without a sufficient water-closet, earth-closet or privy, or without an ashpit furnished with proper doors and coverings, the local authority must, by written notice, require the owner or occupier, within a reasonable time therein specified, to provide the same.

If such notice is not complied with, the local authority may, at the expiration of the time specified in the notice, do the work and recover in a summary manner from the owner the expenses they incur.

By Section 41 a local authority may, on written complaint that any drain, water-closet, earth-closet, privy, ashpit or cesspool is a nuisance or injurious to health (but not otherwise) examine the same, and, if it appears on examination to be in a bad condition or require alteration, the local authority must forthwith cause a notice in writing to be given to the owner or occupier of the premises requiring him to do the necessary works; and if the notice is not complied with the person to whom it is given shall be liable to a penalty of ten shillings a day during default, and the local authority may, if they think fit, execute such works and recover in a summary manner from the owner the expenses incurred.

Generally, by Section 91 any premises in such a state
as to be a nuisance or injurious to health shall be
deemed to be a nuisance liable to be dealt with summarily
in manner provided by the Act. This section applies
to any case where " the premises are decayed,
dilapidated or out of order, as for instance where . . . .
foul matter has been allowed to soak into walls or
floors."[1] By Section 84 the local authority may, on
receipt of any information respecting the existence of
a nuisance, serve a notice on the person by whose act,
default or sufferance the nuisance arises or continues,
or, if such person cannot be found, on either the owner
or the occupier of the premises on which the nuisance
arises, requiring him to abate the same and execute such
works as may be necessary for the purpose. On non-
compliance with notice complaint may be made under
Section 95 to a justice, who shall issue a summons
requiring the person on whom the notice was served to
appear before a court of summary jurisdiction. And
by Section 96 the latter court, if satisfied that the
alleged nuisance exists, or is likely to recur, must make
an order requiring such person to comply with the notice,
or otherwise abate the nuisance, and may in addition
imposed a penalty not exceeding five pounds. Any
person not obeying an order of the court is liable under
Section 98 to a penalty; moreover, the local authority
may enter the premises to which the order relates and
abate the nuisance and recover in a summary manner
the expenses incurred from the person on whom the
order is made.

As to the costs and expenses of the execution of the
above provisions relating to *nuisances,* Section 104 provides that these must be deemed to be money paid for
the use and at the request of the person on whom the

---

[1] R. v. *Purley*, (1889) 22 Q.B.D. 520.

order is made; or if the order is made on the local authority, or if no order is made, but the nuisance is proved to have existed when the complaint was made or the notice given, then of the person by whose act or default the nuisance was caused.

Such costs and expenses, and any penalties incurred in relation to any such nuisance, may be recovered in a summary manner or in any county or superior court; and the court shall have power to divide the liability for them between persons by whose acts or defaults a nuisance is caused in such proportions as to it may seem just.

Any costs and expenses recoverable under this section by a local authority from an owner of premises may be recovered instead from the occupier for the time being of such premises; and the owner must allow such occupier to deduct any money which he pays under this enactment out of his rent.

Nothing in the above-mentioned Act affects any contract between any owner or occupier of any property whereby it may be agreed that the occupier is to discharge all rates dues and sums of money payable in respect of such property, or to affect any contract whatsoever between landlord and tenant.

The result of these provisions may be summarised thus. When premises become so dilapidated as to be injurious to health, the local authority may serve a notice on the owner or occupier. If the notice is not complied with complaint may be made to a justice, and the justice may make an order. If the order is not obeyed the local authority may enter and execute such repairs, as may be necessary to abate the nuisance.

In most cases the notice is served on, and the order made against the owner, and, when this is so, the expenses of executing the repairs will be recoverable from him. Such expenses may, however, be recovered from the tenant who may then deduct what he has been called upon to pay from his rent, provided he is not by the tenancy agreement under an obligation to pay himself.

Where the notice is served on, and the order made against, a tenant the local authority can recover the expenses only from the tenant. Whether the latter can recover what he has paid by deduction from his rent depends again on whether he or the landlord is liable to execute the works having regard to the terms of the tenancy agreement.

Whether the cost of executing works necessary to abate a nuisance is to fall ultimately upon the landlord or upon the tenant depends, therefore, on the terms of the lease or tenancy agreement subsisting between them. Prima facie the landlord is liable, and, if the order is made on the tenant, he can recover the expenses incurred in carrying out its requirements by deduction from the rent. So in one case the Sanitary Authority, acting under Section 4, sub-section 1, of the Public Health (London) Act, 1891, served upon the premises a notice, directed to the owner or occupier, and requiring a nuisance, which arose by reason of water and sewage collecting in the cellar owing to a stoppage in the drains, to be abated. They did not serve on the owner a notice under Section 4, sub-section 3, which provides for the service on the owner of a notice to abate in cases where the nuisance arises from any want or defect of a structural character. The tenant, who held on a yearly tenancy, was liable, under Section 4, sub-section 4, to a penalty of £10 if he made default in complying with the requisitions of the notice, and he therefore did the necessary work, in the course of which it was discovered that the nuisance arose from a structural defect in the drains. He sued the landlord and was successful, the Court holding that he was entitled, under Section 11, sub-section 1, of the Act, to recover from the landlord the costs and expenses incurred in abating the nuisance, as money paid by him " for the use and at the request of " the landlord, although no notice under Section 4, sub-section 3, had been served upon the landlord as owner of the premises. In the opinion of Mr. Justice Charles, the tenant was entitled to recover from the landlord at common law, apart from Section 11, on the principle applicable to cases where one man has been legally compelled to expend money on what another man ought to have done, as in this case the tenant had been legally compelled to incur expense in abating a nuisance which the landlord ought to have abated.[1]

There are at least two ways in which the tenant may be ultimately liable :—

1. The lease or tenancy agreement may contain a covenant by the tenant to repair. If this is so, and if the work required to be done to abate the nuisance consists of repairs which ought, having regard to the terms of the covenant, to have been executed by the tenant, the tenant will be liable. That is to say, if the landlord is compelled by the local authority to pay in the first place, he will be able to recover from the tenant, whereas if the tenant is compelled to pay in the first place, he will not be able, either by deduction from his rent or otherwise, to recover from his landlord.

2. The lease or tenancy agreement may contain a covenant by the tenant to pay " all rates, taxes, assessments, and impositions whatsoever," or in similar

---

[1] *Gebhardt* v. *Saunders*, [1892] 2 Q.B. 452.

terms. The wording of such a covenant may be wide enough to cast upon the tenant an obligation to discharge the expenses involved by obedience to an order.

The first head above involves the question of the nature and extent of the tenant's liability under a repairing covenant, a question which has already been discussed in previous chapters.

Where the work ordered to be done is not repairing work at all, or (and this is more important for the purposes of this book) where the work is repairing work but the lease or tenancy agreement contains no express covenant laying the obligation for such work upon either the landlord or the tenant, the tenant may be liable if, but only if, the lease or tenancy agreement contains a covenant by him to pay rates, taxes, impositions and outgoings in terms wide enough to cover the expenses in question.

It was at one time thought that where a tenant had covenanted to pay all " outgoings " he might nevertheless escape payment of these expenses if he was holding only for a short term or from year to year, and if the expenses were very large in proportion to the rent. The ground for this opinion was that, in such circumstances, it could not have been intended by the parties that such an extraordinary expenditure should be covered by the word, " outgoings." This view, which was contrary to the main current of opinion, was exploded in the recent case of *Lowther* v. *Clifford*[1] in which the cases[2] supporting the view were mentioned with disapproval. In *Lowther* v. *Clifford* a lease had been granted to the defendant for seven years containing a covenant by him to pay " all assessments,

---

[1] (1927) 1 K.B. 130.

[2] *Valpy* v. *St. Leonard's Wharf*, 67 J.P. 402; *Harris* v. *Hickman*, (1904) 1 K.B. 447.

impositions and outgoings now payable or hereafter to become payable by or be imposed upon either landlord or tenant in respect of the premises." The defendant held over at the end of the lease as tenant from year to year. The local authority made up and paved the road upon which the demised land abutted, and demanded and received payment from the plaintiff, the landlord, for the expenses incurred. The plaintiff sought to recover this expenditure from the defendant. Judgment went for the plaintiff. Sargant, L.J., said[1] " The covenant is couched in the widest possible terms, is quite free from ambiguity and obviously includes an imposition or outgoing of the kind in question. And . . . there is not . . . any room for modifying the clear words of the covenant by any consideration based on the length of the term granted by the lease, the condition of the property or the disproportion between the rent reserved and the amount of the imposition in question."

So in a case where a tenant for years had covenanted in his lease to pay " all . . . impositions . . . charged or imposed upon or in respect of the said premises . . . on the landlord, tenant or ocupier of the same," and notice was given to the landlord by the Sanitary Authority under the Public Health (London) Act, 1891, requiring him as owner of the premises to abate a nuisance caused by a privy, and to construct a water-closet in accordance with the bye-laws of the London County Council, it was held that the tenant was liable, under his covenant, to repay the landlord the cost of carrying out the work, such expenses being covered by the word " impositions," and that the obligation was of a class within the contemplation of the parties.[2]

---

[1] At p. 148.
[2] *Foulger* v *Arding*, [1902] 1 K.B. 700.

In another case, where a house was let at the " clear
yearly rent " of £54, under a three years' agreement,
and the tenant had agreed to pay " all rates, taxes,
assessments and impositions whatsoever, whether par-
liamentary, parochial or otherwise, that may become
due or assessed in respect of the . . . premises . . .''
it was held that the expense of complying with a notice
from the Sanitary Authority to reconstruct drains constituted an " imposition " within the agreement for
which the tenant was liable under his contract, notwithstanding the absence of such words as " imposed
on the landlord or tenant," and notwithstanding the
shortness of the tenancy."[1]

So also, where a tenant had taken a house for three
years at the yearly rent of £55, agreeing to pay all
" outgoings in respect of the premises," and during
the tenancy the landlord, in obedience to an order of
the Sanitary Authority, reconstructed the drainage
system of the house at a cost of £83 10s., it was held
that the tenant was liable, under his agreement, to
repay the landlord the amount so expended.[2]

On the other hand, where a tenant covenanted in his
lease " to pay and discharge all . . . assessments,
charges and outgoings whatsoever," but the landlord
covenanted to " keep the exterior of the said dwelling
house and buildings in repair," and the Sanitary
Authority served a notice under the Public Health Act,
1875, on the landlord requiring him to do work which
involved the reconstruction of the drainage system outside the house, it was held that the tenant's covenant

---

[1] *Warriner in re : Brayshaw* v. *Ninnis* [1903] 2 Ch. 367.

[2] *Stockdale* v. *Ascherberg*, [1904] 1 K.B. 447. And see *Bettingham*,
In re : Melhado v. *Woodcock* (1892) 9 T.L.R. 48.

to pay outgoings must be read as being subject to the performance by the landlord of his covenant to repair, and that as the work of reconstruction was necessary in order to enable the landlord to carry out his covenant to repair, the landlord must bear the cost.[1]

A tenant has been held liable for repairing a defective drain required to be repaired by an order of the Local Authority under Section 94 of the Public Health Act, 1875, when, in addition to a covenant to repair, he had agreed to pay " sewers rate and all other taxes, rates, *charges* and assessments whatsoever . . . payable by either the owner or occupier."[2]

Also, under a covenant " to pay and discharge all taxes, rates, *duties* and assessments whatsoever," a tenant was held liable for reconstructing a drain in accordance with requirements of the Local Authority under Section 85 of the Metropolis Management Act, 1855.[3]

Under a similar covenant the tenant was held liable for the cost of connecting the drains of a house with the sewer.[4]

With reference to street paving works executed by the Local Authority under Section 150 of the Public Health Act, 1875, it has been held that a tenant, who has in a twenty-one years' lease covenanted to pay " all rates, taxes and outgoings now payable or hereafter to become payable in respect of the said premises," is liable to repay his landlord who had paid to the Local Authority his proportion of the expenses

---

[1] *Howe* v. *Botwood*, [1913] 2 K.B. 387 ; and compare *Henman* v. *Berliner* [1918] 2 K.B., 236.

[2] *George* v. *Coates*, (1903) 88 L.T, 48.

[3] *Farlow* v. *Stevenson*, [1900] 1 Ch. 128.

[4] *Clayton* v. *Smith*, (1895) 11 T.L.R. 374.

incurred, as such expenses are " *outgoings* payable in respect of the premises."[1] A similar decision was given in an earlier case, where the tenant had in a twenty-one years' lease covenanted to pay " all taxes, charges, rates, duties, tithes and tithe rent-charge assessments and impositions whatever."[2]

But such expenses cannot be recovered by the land-lord from his tenant when the latter has only coven-anted to pay " all *rates, taxes and assessments* what-soever which now are or during the term shall be imposed or assessed upon the premises or the landlords or tenants in respect thereof by authority of Parliament or otherwise, except the landlord's property tax." Such a payment is not a rate, tax or assessment within the meaning of the covenant, and " such covenants as this are confined to rates and assessments of a tem-porary and necessary nature, and do not include a sum which is a charge on property giving it an increased permanent value."[3]

The position may perhaps be summarised thus : " Rates," " taxes," and " assessments," usually refer only to expenses of a temporary or recurring nature, and not to charges giving property an increased per-manent value,[4] and a covenant to pay them does not involve the tenant in liability for expenses incurred in abating a nuisance. On the other hand, a covenant to pay " outgoings " or " impositions " or (perhaps) "charges " will cover such expenses.[5]

---

[1] *Greaves* v. *Whitmarsh, Watson & Co.*, [1906] 2 K.B. 340.

[2] *Wix* v. *Rutson*, [1899] 1 Q.B. 474.

[3] *Baylis* v. *Jiggens*, [1898] 2 Q.B. 315.

[4] *Allum* v. *Dickinson*, 9 Q.B.D. 632 ; and see *Wilkinson* v. *Collyer*, 13 Q.B.D. 1.

[5] There is a dictum to the contrary with regard to "assessments " in *Lowther* v. *Clifford*, (1927) 1 K.B. per Scrutton L. J. at p. 148.

Provisions similar to the above apply to London by virtue of the Public Health (London) Act, 1891.[1]

The sections dealt with in the remainder of this part have been repealed by the Housing Act, 1930, and sections 17-24 of that Act substituted for them. Generally speaking, closing orders may no longer be made. Instead a local authority may serve a notice requiring the execution of specified works necessary to make the house fit for habitation; or, if such works cannot be carried out at reasonable expense, they may order the owner to demolish the house.

Under Section 11 of the Housing Act, 1925, it is the duty of the Local Authority, if satisfied that any dwelling house within their district is in a state so dangerous to health as to be unfit for human habitation, to make an order called a closing order, prohibiting the use of such dwelling house for human habitation until in their judgment it has been rendered fit for that purpose. Notice of the closing order must be served on every owner.[2]

Where the order has become operative the Local Authority must serve a notice of it on every occupier, who must cease to inhabit the house within the period specified in the notice, not being less than fourteen days after service.

If the occupier does not move out of the house within that time, he may be ordered to do so on summary conviction. The exact effect of a closing order on the relationship of landlord and tenant is far from clear. It seems, however, that the tenant has no right to retake possession as soon as the necessary repairs are executed; and, if he does so, he is a trespasser.[3]

---

[1] See Sect. 2 & 4.
[2] *Blake* v. *Smith*, (1921) 2 K.B. 685.
[3] *Blake* v. *Smith* (*supra*).

Unless the house has been made unfit by the wilful act or default of the tenant the Local Authority may make the tenant a reasonable allowance for his expense in removing (the amount to be determined with the consent of the owner or fixed by a Court of summary jurisdiction), and the amount of such allowance is recoverable from the owner.

The Local Authority must determine a closing order made by them when satisfied that the house has been rendered fit for human habitation.

By Section 14 of the Housing Act, 1925, where a closing order has remained operative for three months, the Local Authority must consider the question of the demolition of the house to which it refers. The Local Authority must give every owner notice of the time and place at which this question will be considered, when the owner will be entitled to be heard.

If upon such consideration the Local Authority are of opinion that the house has not been rendered fit, and that necessary steps are not being taken with all due diligence to render it fit, and that the continuance of the house is a nuisance or dangerous to the health of the public or the inhabitants of neigbouring houses, they must order its demolition, subject to postponement on terms set out in the Act.

The Local Authority has no discretion in the matter, but is under a duty to make the order.[1]

By Section 3 of the Housing Act, 1925, if the owner of a house suitable for occupation by the working classes fails to make or keep the hcuse in all respects reasonably fit for human habitation the Local Authority may serve the owner a notice requiring him within a

---

[1] *Lancaster* v. *Burnley Corporation*, (1915) 1 K.B. 259.

reasonable time, not being less than 21 days, to execute such works as may be necessary for that purpose. This section applies whether the house is let or not let, and the limitations as to rent contained in Section 1 are not incorporated.[1]

The notice must specify what works are to be executed as being necessary to make the house in all respects reasonably fit for human habitation; and in addition to serving the notice on the owner the Local Authority may serve copies of the notice on any persons having an estate or interest in the premises superior to that of the owner.

The owner may appeal to the Minister of Health, by giving notice of appeal to him within twenty-one days, against the notice by the Local Authority requiring him to execute the work, and no proceedings are to be taken by the Local Authority while the appeal is pending.

If the work specified in the notice by the Local Authority is not done, then, if there has been no appeal, at the expiration of the time limited by the notice to execute the works, or if there has been an unsuccessful appeal after the expiration of 21 days, the Local Authority may itself do the work.

It may then demand the expenses of doing the work together with the current rate of interest thereon from the owner. If he fails to pay, the Local Authority may recover the expenses and interest either by proceedings in a court of summary jurisdiction, or by exercising any or all the powers given to a mortgagee having a power of sale, lease, accepting surrenders of leases and appointing a receiver, by the Conveyancing Acts 1881 to 1922.

---

[1] *Arlidge* v. *Tottenham*, [1922] 2 K.B. 710.

The owner may appeal to the Minister of Health against the demand, but he cannot raise any question, such as the necessity of the work, which might have been raised on an appeal against the notice to execute the work.

If the house is not capable of being rendered fit for human habitation without *reconstruction,* the owner may declare his intention of closing it, and a closing order shall then be deemed to have been made in respect of it.

PART 2.—PROVISIONS DESIGNED TO PROMOTE PUBLIC SAFETY.

Under Section 160 of the Public Health Act, 1875,[1] Sections 75-78 of the Towns Improvement Clauses Act, 1847,[2] are incorporated. These provisions, which apply outside the London area, are shortly as follows : If any building or wall is ruinous or dangerous, the surveyor shall cause a proper hoarding to be put up to protect passers by, and shall give notice to the owner and to the occupier to take down, secure or repair such building or wall. If the repairs, etc., are not done, complaint may be made to two Justices, who may order the owner, and, failing him, the occupier, to do the necessary work within a specified time; and, in default, the Local Authority may do the work, and recover the cost from the owner, by distress if necessary. If the owner cannot be found, the Local Authority may, after due notice, take such building or land, making compensation to the owner as provided by the Lands Clauses Act, 1845,[3] in the case of land taken otherwise than with the consent of the owner. If such house is pulled down they may sell the materials, paying the owner the overplus arising from the sale, after deducting the expenses incurred.

---

[1] 38 & 39 Vict., c. 55.

[2] 10 & 11 Vict., c. 34.

[3] 8 Vict., c. 18.

Similar provisions are made for the London area by Part IX of the London Building Act, 1894, as amended (with regard to the service of notices) by Section 5 of the London Building (Amendment) Act, 1898.[1] It enacts that whenever it becomes known to the London County Council that any structure is in a dangerous state, they shall require such structure to be surveyed by the district surveyor, or some other competent surveyor, who shall thereupon make a report to them.

If the building is certified to be in a dangerous state, the Council may thereupon cause the same to be shored up, or otherwise secured, and a fence put round it, and shall serve a notice on the owner or occupier, or some person on the premises, or fix a copy of such notice on the premises requiring him forthwith to take down, secure or repair the structure, as may be necessary.

If the owner or occupier to whom notice is given pays no attention to the notice, the Council must make complaint before a magistrate, who may order the owner to take down or repair the building, etc., within a specified time, and if at the expiration of such time the order has not been complied with, the Council may do the required work and charge the owner with the cost, including the cost of obtaining the order, without prejudice to the owner's right to recover the same from the tenant or any other person who is under obligation to repair.

If the owner cannot be found, or on the owner's default or refusal to pay such expenses, the Council, after serving him with three months' notice of their intention to do so, may sell such structure to pay the expenses, paying the surplus (if any) after deducting the expenses incurred, to the owner on demand. If

---

[1] 61 & 62 Vict., c. cxxxvii.

the proceeds of the sale are insufficient, the Council may recover the balance from the owner by proceedings before a magistrate under the Summary Jurisdiction Acts.

The expression " owner," under the London Building Act, 1894, Section 5 (29), applies to every person in possession or receipt either of the whole or of any part of the rents or profits of any land or tenement, or in the occupation of any land or tenement, *otherwise than as a tenant from year to year, or any less term, or as a tenant at will.* Therefore, any tenant under a three years' agreement or a lease for a term of years will be liable as " owner," as also will be a tenant in possession of *part* of a house under an agreement or lease for a greater interest than from year to year, or a tenant of a house for a term of years who has under-let parts of it.

In order to facilitate the recovery of expenses under the Act, by Section 173 " the owner immediately entitled in possession, *or the occupier,*" shall in the first instance pay the expenses, with this limitation, that an occupier shall not be liable to pay any sum exceeding in amount the rent due, or which will afterwards become due, from him in respect of the premises. Also any occupier who has paid such expenses may deduct the amount so paid from any rent payable by him to any owner of the same premises, and any owner who has paid more than his due proportion of any such expenses may deduct the amount so overpaid from any rent payable by him to any other owner of the same premises, or he can recover the amount by action.

It should be noted, however, that the word " occupier " only applies to tenants holding from year to year or for shorter periods, since a tenant for a longer period comes within the definition of " owner."

Any owner or other person authorised by him may, under Section 192, enter any premises for the purpose of complying with any notice or order served or made on him under this Act, after giving seven days' notice to the occupier, and on producing the notice or order.

By Section 35 of the Public Health Acts Amendment Act,[1] 1890, all vaults, arches and cellars under any street, and all openings into them in the surface of any street, and all cellar-heads, gratings, lights and coal-holes must be kept in good condition and repair by the owners or occupiers of the same or of the houses or buildings to which the same respectively belong. In case of disrepair the Urban Authority may, after twenty-four hours' notice, do the necessary repairs, and the expenses of so doing shall be paid to the Urban Authority by such owner or occupier.

Under Section 19 of the Public Health Acts Amendment Act, 1907,[2] in the event of a private street being out of repair, and likely to be dangerous to foot passengers or vehicles, the Local Authority may require the frontagers to repair the street within a specified time, failing which the Local Authority may execute the repairs and recover the cost from the owners.

By Section 30, if in any situation adjoining a public street or footpath, any building, wall, fence, structure or other thing, or any well, excavation, reservoir, pond, etc., is, owing to want of sufficient repair, protection or enclosure, dangerous to the public, the Local Authority may require the owner to repair, remove, protect or enclose the same, so as to prevent any danger, and, if he fails to do so, the Local Authority may do the work and recover the cost from the owner.[3]

---

[1] 53 & 54 Vict., c. 59 (an adoptive Act).

[2] 7 Edw. 7, c. 53 (an adoptive Act).

[3] For definition of "owner," see Public Health Act, 1875, (38 & 39 Vict., c. 55) s. 4.

CHAPTER IX.

LIABILITY FOR DILAPIDATIONS OF FENCES AND PARTY WALLS.

PART 1.—FENCES.

WHEN a man makes a ditch as a boundary between his neighbour's land and his own, he must not, of course, cut into his neighbour's land, for that would be a trespass. He usually cuts to the extreme edge of his own land, however, so that the far side of the ditch coincides with his boundary line. He must not throw the soil that he digs in making the ditch on his neighbour's land so he usually banks it up on his own side of the ditch, and sometimes plants a hedge or makes a fence upon the top of it. This procedure is so common throughout the country that the law has taken judicial cognizance of it, and whenever there is a boundary consisting of a ditch and hedge there is a presumption of fact that both ditch and hedge belong to the owner of the field on the hedge side of the boundary. This presumption of fact may be rebutted by appropriate evidence to the contrary, but it will require strong evidence of actual title to the strip of land in order to do so.

So in *Henniker* v. *Howard*[1] the plaintiff and defendant were adjoining owners of land, the lands being bounded by a bank with a fence and with a ditch on the defendant's side. The defendant had, for nearly fifty years repaired and trimmed the fence, pollarded the trees, and cleared the ditch, but there was no evidence of knowledge of this on the part of the

---

[1] (1904) 90 L.T. 157.

plaintiff. In the absence of such knowledge it was held that these acts of ownership did not rebut the presumption that the bank and fence were the property of the plaintiff.

Where there are two fences, one on each side of a ditch, or two ditches, one on each side of a bank or fence, or a fence without any ditch there is no presumption as to the ownership, and it must be proved either by strict proof of title or by showing long continued acts of ownership. If both the adjoining owners exercised these acts of ownership with the knowledge of the other, they will be tenants in common of that part of the boundary.

In the absence of evidence to the contrary, however, a fence made of oak or other wood pales belongs to the owner on whose side are the horizontal rails to which the pales are nailed. In other words, it is presumed that an owner in erecting a fence drives in the nails so that the points are towards his own land.

As between a landlord and his tenant the liability to repair fences falls upon the tenant even in the absence of any express covenant in the lease to that effect.[1] This obligation arises from the duty of a tenant to preserve the boundaries of the demised premises. If, however, the landlord has undertaken to keep the premises in repair, he will be liable to repair the fences.

If two persons possess adjoining fields, neither of them is, apart from agreement, under any obligation to the other to fence. But each is liable if his cattle enter upon the land of the other. There is no obligation on adjoining occupiers, as between themselves,

---

[1] *Cheetham* v. *Hampson*, (1791) 4 T.R. 318.

to fence, even where the tenant of each field has, as between himself and a common landlord, covenanted to keep the fences dividing the fields in good repair. Therefore, if, in the latter case, one tenant fails to maintain a fence so that the cattle of the other strays on to his land and does damage, he can nevertheless recover against the other for allowing the cattle to trespass in spite of his failure to keep his covenant with his landlord.[1] The principle applied in such case being that the owners of cattle must keep them upon their land at their peril.[2]

Railway companies are, under the provisions of the Railway Clauses Act, 1845,[3] bound to make and maintain fences between their railway and adjoining lands, for protecting such adjoining lands, and for preventing the cattle of adjoining owners from straying on to the railway.

Under the Public Health Acts Amendment Act 1907,[4] s. 31, if any land (other than a common) adjoining a street is unfenced, or if the fences are out of repair, and such land, owing to the non-repair of the fence, is a source of danger to passengers, or is used for any immoral or indecent purposes, or for any purpose causing annoyance or inconvenience to the public, the Local Authority may serve a notice on the owner or occupier requiring the land to be fenced or the fence repaired; and if this is not done within fourteen days, the Local Authority may do the necessary work, and recover the cost from the owner or occupier.

---

[1] *Holgate* v. *Bleazard*, [1917] 1 K.B. 443.
[2] *Ibid. and Cf. Fletcher* v. *Rylands*, (1868), L.R. 3 H.L. 330.
[3] 8 Vict., c. 20, s. 68.
[4] 7 Edw. VII., c. 53.

PART 2.—PARTY WALLS.

Before 1926 the expression " party wall " was used in four different senses : (1) A wall of which the two adjoining owners are tenants in common—this was the most usual and the primary meaning of the term. Thus if two adjoining houses with a party wall were conveyed to different people, and in the deeds the common wall was expressed to be conveyed as a "party" wall, this was construed so as to make the adjoining owners tenants in common of the wall.[1] (2) A wall the ownership of which is divided longitudinally into two strips, one belonging to each of the adjoining owners. (3) A wall which belongs entirely to one of the adjoining owners, but is subject to an easement in the other to have it maintained as a dividing wall between the two tenements. (4) A wall divided longitudinally into two moieties, each moiety being subject to a cross easement in favour of the owner of the other moiety. Now by the Law of Property Act (1st Schedule, Part V), all party walls of type (1) existing on 1st January, 1926, are converted into party walls of type (4), and by Section 38 an attempt to create a party wall of type (1) will after 1925 operate to create one of type (4).

When a party wall is built by two owners, part of the wall being on one owner's land and part on the land of the other, it is a party wall of type (2) and each owner owns that part of the wall which is on his own land. But if the boundary between the two adjoining lands cannot be accurately determined so that it cannot be ascertained how much of the wall is on the land of each, the party wall is presumed to be of type (4); the boundary is presumed to be in the middle of the wall, and each owner owns one

---

[1] *Watson* v. *Gray*, (1880) 14 Ch. D. 192, per Fry, J.

half of the wall subject to cross easements of support.
If the wall is entirely on the land of one of the adjoining
owners, it is, of course, entirely his wall, but it may
be subject to an easement of support in favour of the
adjoining owner, in which case it is a party wall of
type (3). Such an easement may be created by express
or implied grant or by prescription. If the wall is of
type (2) and each of the adjoining owners owns that part
on his own land in severalty, each part may be subject
to an easement of support in favour of the other as in
type (4). But the common user by the adjoining
owners of a wall between their property, in the absence
of proof of ownership of the particular land on which
it is built, did not before 1926 give cross easements of
this type by prescription but raises a presumption that
the wall is of type (1). After 1925 cross easements will
be implied.

The law as to the liability to repair a party wall of
type (1), *i.e.*, when the owners own it as tenants in common was not very clear, and, as a result of the provisions
of the Law of Property Act referred to above, is now of
historical interest only. In an American case *Campbell*
v. *Mesier*[1] (quoted in *Leigh* v. *Dickeson*[2]), where an
owner had pulled down his house, and also the party
wall of type (1), which had become ruinous, and then
rebuilt the party wall, it was held that the adjoining
owner was bound to contribute rateably to the expense
of the new wall, it being absolutely necessary to have
the wall rebuilt. An adjoining owner is not, however,
bound to contribute towards building the new wall
higher than the old, nor, if materials more costly or of
a different nature are used, is he bound to pay any part
of the extra expense.

---

[1] (1820) 4 John (Amer. Ch.) 334.
[2] (1883) 12 Q.B.D. 194.

As regards walls of type (2) neither is, of course, under any liability to repair his wall for the benefit of the other. If he desires to do so, he may pull down his portion of the wall, even though he does not thereby leave sufficient support for the other owner's part.[1] He need not give notice to the other of his intention so to do, nor need he provide any facilities for the other to shore up his wall.[2] But he must do the work of tearing down his wall in a proper, careful and workmanlike manner or he will be liable for all the damage caused to the other. In types (3) and (4), and since 1925 in type (1), which has, as we have seen, been assimilated with type (4), when one of the adjoining owners has an easement of support, or both have such an easement, the other must, of course, at all times furnish such support, and if necessary must repair the wall in order to do so. If the other wishes to tear down the wall in type (3) or his part of the wall in type (4) he is bound to shore up the wall in such a way that the easement of support is not interfered with.

In connection with party walls and structures inside the London area it is necessary to consider some of the provisions of the London Building Act, 1894.[3]

Under Part VIII of that Act provision is made with respect to party structures which the owner of one house wishes to repair or improve. Such an owner is termed under the Act the " building owner "; the owner of the adjoining house is called the " adjoining owner." A building owner has, by virtue of Section 88, shortly, the following rights in regard to a party structure :—

(1.) To make good, underpin or repair any party structure defective or out of repair.

---

[1] *Wigford* v. *Gill* Cro., Eliz. 269 ; *Cubitt* v. *Porter* 8 B. & C. 257.

[2] *Chadwick* v. *Trower*, 6 Bing. N.C.1.

[3] 57 & 58 Vict., c. ccxiii.

(2.) To pull down and rebuild any such structure which is so far defective or out of repair as to make it necessary to pull it down.

(3.) To raise and underpin party structures, if permitted by the Act, or any external wall built against any such party structure, provided he makes good any damage occasioned thereby to the adjoining owner, and carries up the flues and chimney stacks belonging to the adjoining owner to a proper height.

Generally, the building owner may pull down any party structure not strong enough to carry any building intended to be erected. He may cut into a party structure. He may cut away projections from any party wall. He may, in order to erect an upright wall against it, take down or cut away any part of a wall which overhangs his ground.

All these rights may be exercised, provided the building owner makes good any damage occasioned to the adjoining premises by reason of such work. He may also carry out any works necessary to connect the party structure with the adjoining premises.

Whenever the building owner proposes to exercise any of the rights conferred upon him with respect to party structures, the adjoining owner may, by notice in writing, require him to build on the party structure such chimney jambs, breasts or flues, piers, recesses or like conveniences as may fairly be required for the convenience of such adjoining owner, unless compliance with such request will cause the building owner unnecessary inconvenience, injury or delay; and if the adjoining owner contests the point, this like other differences, must be settled by arbitration.

Before a building owner commences any work on a party structure, unless the adjoining owner and occupiers consent in writing to the work being proceeded with, or the building is dangerous, he must give at least two months' notice to the adjoining owner, and this notice must be either personal or must be sent in a registered letter to the owner at his last known place of abode, or delivered to some person on the premises, or if no person be found on the premises, a copy of the notice may be fixed thereto in a conspicuous position. The notice must be either printed or in writing; it must state the nature of the proposed works, and the time when it is proposed to commence such works.

Unless the party structure had been condemned by the district surveyor, the onus of proving it to be dangerous would, doubtless, rest on the building owner.

The adjoining owner, on receiving such notice, may require the building owner to build, or may himself build, on such party structure, any of the works previously described. He must send to the building owner, within one month from the receipt of the " party-wall notice," a notice in which he must specify the work he requires to be done, and also give any necessary plans. If either owner does not, within fourteen days from the service on him of any notice, express his consent thereto, a difference shall be deemed to have arisen between the building owner and the adjoining owner. In the case of a difference arising, both parties may agree upon a surveyor to determine it, or each party may appoint a surveyor, and the two surveyors shall appoint a third surveyor. These three surveyors, or any two of them, may determine the difference. They may by their award determine the right to do the work, the time and manner of doing it, and any other matter that arises out of the subject in difference, but, unless otherwise agreed, the time fixed for beginning the works shall not be until after the expiration of the before-mentioned notice. In practice, however, it is usual to agree to commence the works at once. The award may be appealed against to the County Court at any time within fourteen days from the date of the delivery thereof.

If either party fails to appoint a surveyor within ten days of the notice requiring him to do so, the party serving the notice may make the appointment.

The costs of preparing the award shall be paid by such party as the surveyors shall determine.

Section 95 deals with the expenses of work to party structures. Shortly, its provisions are as follows :—

(1.) All expenses of repairing or rebuilding defective party structures are to be borne by building and adjoining owners in proportion to the use that each owner makes or may make of such structure. Thus, the adjoining owner will have to bear the cost of any extra works which he requires the building owner to execute for the adjoining owner's convenience.

(2.) The same principle applies to pulling down any timber or other partition dividing a building, and building a party wall in its stead.

(3.) The building owner must bear the whole cost of raising a party structure or any external wall built against another external wall for his own convenience, and the cost of carrying up the flues and chimneys of the adjoining owner to the requisite height on or against such party structure or external wall. He must also bear the whole cost of pulling down and rebuilding for his own convenience any party structures which are sound and of proper material. He must bear the cost of cutting into and repairing any party structure so cut into. He must also bear the cost of cutting away and making good any footing, chimney breast, jambs or floors cut away, and he must pay the adjoining owner compensation for disturbance and inconvenience caused by the works.

By Section 92 a building owner and his workmen may, after giving the owner and occupier fourteen days' notice (or, in a case of emergency, reasonable notice), enter any premises for the purpose of executing any work which he is entitled to execute, and may remove furniture, etc. If the premises are closed, he may, if accompanied by a policeman, break open any fences or doors for this purpose.

The building owner shall, within one month after the completion of any works the expenses of which are partly to be borne by the adjoining owner, or of any works executed at the request of the adjoining owner, deliver to such owner an account in writing of the particulars and expenses of such work, after allowing credit for old materials. The adjoining owner may state his objections to such account within a month after receiving it, and any dispute shall be settled by arbitration.

CHAPTER X.

LIABILITY FOR ECCLESIASTICAL DILAPIDATIONS.

IN the case of ecclesiastical dilapidations, the incumbent has, of course, no liability in respect of covenants, since there is no landlord, the freehold of the property belonging to the incumbent so long as he remains in that position. However, upon the principle that " he should endure the burden who derives the advantage," the incumbent, or after his death his personal representatives, was or were liable at Common Law for the repair and renewal of buildings, the income derived from the benefice being the only fund available for repairs or rebuilding.

An incumbent is at common law bound to maintain the parsonage and also the chancel (unless it is the custom for the parishioners to keep this in repair), and "keep them in good and substantial repair, restoring and rebuilding when necessary, according to the original form, without addition or modern improvement; and he is not bound to supply or maintain anything in the nature of ornament, to which painting (unless necessary to preserve exposed timbers from decay) and white-washing and papering belong."[1]

His position is closely akin to that of a tenant for life, with two important differences. First by the Common Law he is liable for permissive as well as voluntary waste. Secondly, until 1871, when the Ecclesiastical Dilapidations Measure was passed, the incumbent could not be made liable for any repairs

---

[1] Per Bailey, J., in *Wise* v. *Metcalf*, (1829) 10 B. & C., at p. 316.

while actually holding the living. Action could be taken only by the successor of an incumbent against either the incumbent who had retired, or the personal representatives of an incumbent who had died. The position therefore was that, although the liability was clear, the means of enforcing it were imperfect. The Ecclesiastical Dilapidations Act, 1871, did something to rectify this, and that Act has been replaced[1] by much more comprehensive legislation, the Ecclesiastical Dilapidations Measure, 1923, as amended by the Ecclesiastical Dilapidations (Amendment) Measure, 1929. The main purpose of these Measures seems to be to set up an authority which *viz-a-viz* the incumbent will occupy a position similar to that occupied by the landlord, *viz-a-viz* his tenant where the lease contains repairing covenants by the latter. The material sections of these Measures are set out in the Appendix where they can be studied by those particularly interested in the subject. What follows is a short summary of their main provisions.

In each diocese an authority known as the Diocesan Dilapidations Board is set up by the Diocesan Conference, and this Board appoints a number of surveyors to act as Diocesan Surveyors. The first duty of the Board is to cause what are called first inspections of the buildings of each benefice in the diocese. By the buildings of a benefice are meant all such houses of residence, glebe buildings, walls, fences and other buildings as the incumbent is by law or custom bound to maintain in repair. Subsequently the Board causes a quinquennial inspection to be carried out. These inspections are made by the diocesan surveyors.

[1] And repealed except for Sections 25, 26, 27 and 28 which deal with repairs to the residences of Archbishops, Bishops, Deans and Canons.

On each inspection the surveyor makes a report to
the Board stating :—

(1.) What immediate repairs are necessary.

(2.) Within what time (not exceeding one year) they ought to
be executed.

(3.) Their cost.

(4.) Assuming the immediate repairs to have been executed
what sum will be necessary to meet the probable cost of
repairs (called quinquennial repairs) which will require
to be executed during the next five years.

(5.) What additional sum is necessary to meet the probable
cost of future repairs (called deferred repairs) for the
carrying out of which during a period exceeding five years
it is, in the opinion of the surveyor, desirable to provide
a fund.

It will at once be asked, what standard is a surveyor
to adopt in deciding whether to include in his report
a particular repair ?   Little guidance on this important
question is to be found in the Measures.   It is laid
down that the surveyor's report is to be " based on
the obligation on the person lawfully bound to keep
or have kept the buildings in good and substantial
repair."   The surveyors employed will no doubt in
practice have been accustomed chiefly to dealing with
repairs as between landlord and tenant, and will be
disposed to adopt as their standard the obligation of a
tenant under a repairing covenant to keep in good and
substantial repair.   It is submitted that the words quoted
from the Measure show that the surveyor is intended
to adopt such a standard.

Having decided that a certain repair must be included
in his report, because it is a repair for which a tenant
would be liable under a covenant to put and keep in
good and substantial repair, the surveyor must decide
whether to classify the repair as immediate, quinquennial or deferred.   On what principle is he to decide
this question ?   Here again not much guidance is to
be found in the Measures.   With some hesitation it

is submitted that repairs which are necessary to *put* the buildings into good and substantial repair must be classed as either immediate or deferred, while repairs which will be necessary to *keep* the buildings in good and substantial repair must be classed as quinquennial. With regard to the first class, repairs necessary to put the buildings into good and substantial repair, a repair will probably be classed as deferred if it involves the execution of extensive work, and if it can safely be postponed without risk of the dilapidation injuriously affecting the state of the building as a whole. Thus the foundations of a building may require strengthening, before it can be said with complete truth to be in a state of good and substantial repair. But the surveyor may be of opinion that the work may be postponed for five years or more without the weakness in the foundations affecting the state of repair of the other parts of the building. In such circumstances the surveyor would, it is suggested, be justified in classifying the strengthening of the foundations as a deferred repair. Repairs required to put the buildings in repair which are small (such as renewal of window sashes) or require to be carried out at once to avoid the immediate development of further dilapidations (such as the replacement of a useless roof) will no doubt be classed in the report as immediate repairs. Recurring repairs (such as painting and pointing) which will fall to be done during the next five years after his report, to maintain the buildings in the required condition, will be classified as quinquennial repairs.

The report of the surveyor is submitted to the Diocesan Dilapidations Board who, after hearing any objections which the incumbent may see fit to make thereto, may make an order confirming the report either with or without modification.

A copy of the order is sent to the incumbent, and
to the Central Authority, Queen Anne's Bounty.

So much for the method by which it is decided what
repairs must be done. The Measure next makes provision for their execution and cost. The general
scheme of the Measure compels the incumbent to pay
sums to the Central Authority and empowers the Central
Authority first to order the incumbent to carry out
specified repairs and secondly to pay for them out of
the sums so received.

When a first inspection is carried out the incumbent
must at once pay to the Central Authority the amount
mentioned in the order as being the cost of the immediate
repairs.

In all other cases, that is in all cases of subsequent
inspections, and in the case of a first inspection in respect
of quinquennial and deferred repairs, the Central
Authority, as soon as the copy of the order is received
makes what is called an " Ordinary Assessment," and if
necessary, a " Long Assessment " as well. The Ordinary Assessment fixes an annual payment to be made by
the incumbent to the Central Authority for the next
quinquennial period in respect of repairs. The annual
payment includes a sum sufficient in the opinion of the
Central Authority to meet the cost of all repairs required
by the order of the Board except deferred repairs and
immediate repairs, the cost of which is ordered to
be paid at once on a first inspection. Repairs, the cost
of which is included in an Ordinary Assessment are,
therefore : —

(1.) On a first inspection the quinquennial repairs.
(2.) On a subsequent inspection both the ordinary and the
        quinquennial repairs.

At the same time the Central Authority may make in
respect of deferred repairs, if there are any, a Long

Assessment similar to the Ordinary Assessment except that payment is spread over a longer period than five years.

The payments required by the Ordinary and Long Assessments are made to the Central Authority by the incumbent and paid by them into a special account called " The Repair Account of the Benefice of . . . ." and " The Deferred Repair Account of the Benefice of . . . ." respectively.

Finally, the Diocesan Dilapidations Board is empowered to order an incumbent to execute specified repairs, and the incumbent must obey the order provided that the obligation of the incumbent is limited to the amounts respectively standing to the credit of the above accounts at the time when the order is made together with any amounts then owing by the incumbent to the accounts. The cost of the repairs is discharged out of the accounts.

Two further provisions of the Measures require notice :—

(1.) The incumbent is relieved from liability to repair the chancel of the church, and the liability is placed upon the person or persons (generally the churchwardens provided they can procure the necessary funds for the purpose) who are responsible for the repair of the rest of the church.

(2.) The surveyor may report to the Board that a building is superfluous, or the incumbent may represent to the Board that a building is superfluous, whereupon the Board may, with the consent of the patron and incumbent, order its removal. This provision may have the effect of relieving the incumbent of the burden, in some cases a very heavy one, of keeping in repair buildings for which he can find no use at all in the present changed conditions.

CHAPTER XI.

LIABILITY FOR AGRICULTURAL DILAPIDATIONS.

THE general law relating to waste and the dilapidation of buildings is as applicable to an agricultural as any other tenancy. By reason, however, of some of the provisions of the Agricultural Holdings Act, 1923, affecting the respective rights and liabilities of land-lords and tenants of agricultural holdings, it is desir-able to state shortly some of the peculiar characteristics of such tenancies. Moreover, amongst agricultural people, the term "dilapidations" is often used to include not only dilapidations to buildings but also dilapidations to land, which gives the word a more extended meaning than that in which it is used else-where in this book. Dilapidations to land include all acts contrary to contract or custom which are detri-mental to the land from a farming point of view.

Corresponding to the implied liability resting upon every tenant of a building to use the same in a tenant-like manner, there is an implied obligation on the part of every agricultural tenant to use and cultivate his farm in a husband-like manner according to the custom of the country. And an action will lie against a tenant for breach of covenant to cultivate in a good and husband-like manner, upon evidence that he has treated the land contrary to the course of good husbandry prevalent in that neighbourhood, if the holding has been thereby injured or deteriorated. So the tenant must observe the ordinary rules of rotation of cropping, cleanse and scour the ditches, and repair fences.[1] Moreover, where at the beginning of the tenancy the land is below proper

---

[1] See Ante p. 119.

condition the tenant does not fulfil his obligation by leaving it in the same condition as that in which he found it. If proper farming during the tenancy will restore the farm to its proper condition, the landlord is entitled to have it delivered up at the end of the term in that condition.[1]

By the Agricultural Holdings Act, 1923, both the landlord and the tenant, in addition to the rights which they may have against one another by virtue of the lease or tenancy agreement subsisting between them, are given a statutory right to compensation at the end of the tenancy in respect of various matters. The compensation is determined by arbitration. An exhaustive discussion of all the cases in which a right to compensation arises is obviously outside the scope of this book. Only three need be mentioned here as affecting the law of dilapidations. The first two relate to what has been called above dilapidations to land, and the third to dilapidations to buildings.

1.   COMPENSATION TO LANDLORD FOR DILAPIDATIONS TO LAND.

Section 10 of the Agricultural Holdings Act, 1923, provides as follows :—

" Where a landlord proves, to the satisfaction of an arbitrator appointed under this Act, on the termination of the tenancy of a holding, that the value of the holding has been deteriorated during the tenancy by the failure of the tenant to cultivate the holding according to the rules of good husbandry or the terms of the contract of tenancy, the arbitrator shall award to the landlord such compensation as in his opinion represents the deterioration of the holding due to such failure :

Provided that—

  (a) compensation shall not be payable under this section unless the landlord has, before the termination of the tenancy, given notice in writing to the tenant of his intention to claim such compensation ; and

---

[1] *Williams* v. *Lewis*, [1915] 3 K.B. 493.

(*b*) nothing in this section shall prevent a landlord from claiming compensation for dilapidations or for the deterioration of the holding under the contract of tenancy."

For the purposes of the above provisions Section 57 (1) of the Act of 1923 provides that :

" Rules of good husbandry " means (due regard being had to the character of the holding) so far as is practicable having regard to its character and position—

(*a*) the maintenance of the land (whether arable, meadow, or pasture), clean and in a good state of cultivation and fertility, and in good condition ; and

(*b*) the maintenance and clearing of drains, embankments, and ditches ; and

(*c*) the maintenance and proper repair of fences, stone walls, gates, and hedges; and

(*d*) the execution of repairs to buildings, being repairs which are necessary for the proper cultivation and working of the land on which they are to be executed ; and

(*e*) such rules of good husbandry as are generally recognised as applying to holdings of the same character and in the same neighbourhood as the holding in respect of which the expression is to be applied :

Provided that the foregoing definition shall not imply an obligation on the part of any person to maintain or clear drains, embankment, or ditches, if and so far as the execution of the works required is rendered impossible (except at prohibitive or unreasonable expense) by reason of subsidence of any land or the blocking of outfalls which are not under the control of that person, or in its application to land in the occupation of a tenant imply an obligation on the part of the tenant—

(i) to maintain or clear drains, embankments, or ditches, or to maintain or properly repair fences, stone walls, gates, or hedges where such work is not required to be done by him under his contract of tenancy ; or

(ii) to execute repairs to buildings which are not required to be executed by him under his contract of tenancy :

And it is further provided by Section 57 (3) of the Act that :

" References to the terms, conditions, or requirements of a contract of tenancy of or of an agreement relating to a holding shall be construed as including references to any obligations, conditions, or liabilities implied by the custom of the country in respect of the holding."

With regard to the notice which the landlord is required to give to the tenant of his intention to make the claim for the compensation given by these provisions, there is no requirement as to its contents, and, as long as it is in writing and contains a clear expression of intention to make such a claim, any form would appear sufficient. There appears to be no necessity to give in this notice any details of the claim, nor to state any amount. And it can apparently be given at any time before the termination of the tenancy.

But particulars of the claim will have to be given before the expiration of two months from the end of the tenancy, otherwise the claim will cease to be enforceable under Section 16 of the Act of 1923.

If the details are available at the time, there is no reason why the notice of intention to claim and the particulars should not be combined in one form, and given to the tenant before the termination of the tenancy.

It will be observed that the above provisions do not take away the landlord's right to claim against a tenant for waste, or a breach of the terms (express or implied)[1] of the contract of tenancy, and it is difficult to say whether the provisions in any way extend such common law rights. It may be useful to note that the latter may still be enforced although there has been no notice of intention to do so given before the termination of the tenancy, for such a notice is only required for claims made under the section.[2] But even claims for waste and breaches of the terms of the contract of tenancy must now be referred to arbitration,[3] and

---

[1] *Arden v. Rutter*, [1923] W.N. 218.

[2] *Ibid.*

[3] Agricultural Holdings Act, 1923, s. 16 (1).

cease to be enforceable after two months from the termination of the tenancy, unless particulars thereof have been given by the landlord to the tenant before the expiration of that period.[1]

2. COMPENSATION TO TENANT FOR SPECIAL STANDARD OR SYSTEM OF FARMING.

This case is in some respects the converse of that last considered.

The Agriculture Act, 1920, for the first time gave consideration to the general improvement in the condition of a holding resulting from a tenant's standard or system of farming. Previously, compensation was restricted to the specific improvements scheduled in the Acts; but now, in certain circumstances, compensation may be recovered where the tenant's standard or system of farming has increased the value of the holding.

The provisions of the above Act have been repealed and re-enacted by Section 9 of the Agricultural Holdings Act, 1923, which now provides as follows :—

" (1) Where a tenant on quitting a holding proves to the satisfaction of an arbitrator appointed under this Act that the value of the holding to an incoming tenant has been increased during the tenancy by the continuous adoption of a standard of farming or a system of farming which has been more beneficial to the holding than the standard or system (if any) required by the contract of tenancy, the arbitrator shall award to the tenant such compensation as in his opinion represents the value to an incoming tenant of the adoption of that standard or system :

Provided that—

 (a) this section shall not apply in any case unless a record of the condition of the holding has been made under this Act, or any enactment repealed by this Act, or in respect of any matter arising before the date of the record so made ; and

---

[1] Agricultural Holdings Act, 1923, s. 16 (2) ; but note S. 30 (2).

(b) compensation shall not be payable under this section unless the tenant has, before the termination of the tenancy, given notice in writing to the landlord of his intention to claim such compensation; and

(c) the arbitrator in assessing the value to an incoming tenant shall make due allowance for any compensation agreed or awarded to be paid to the tenant for any improvement specified in the First Schedule to this Act which has caused or contributed to the benefit.

(2) Nothing in this section shall entitle a tenant to recover in respect of an improvement specified in the First Schedule or the Third Schedule to this Act any compensation which he would not have been entitled to recover if this section had not been passed.

* * * * *

The above requires the standard or system adopted by the tenant to be compared with the standard or system (if any) required by his contract of tenancy. The latter may contain an express covenant requiring some definite standard or system, in which case the arbitrator will make that his basis for comparison. But if there is no such express covenant, the law implies a covenant on the part of the tenant to cultivate the land in a good and husband-like manner according to the custom of the country, and to continue to do so down to the termination of his tenancy;[1] and, it is submitted, the arbitrator should in such latter case make the requirements of the implied covenant the basis for his comparison.

3. COMPENSATION TO TENANT FOR SPECIFIC IMPROVEMENTS TO THE HOLDING.

By the Act of 1923, which consolidates a number of previous Acts, the tenant of an agricultural holding is given a right to claim from his landlord at the termination of the tenancy compensation in respect of a large

---

[1] See *Williams* v. *Lewis*, [1915] 3 K.B., p. 494; and Agricultural Holdings Act, 1923, s. 57 (3).

variety of improvements made by him during the tenancy. Apart from the provisions of these Acts, the benefit of such improvements would pass to the landlord on the principle that whatever is attached to the soil passes with the soil.

The general scheme of the Act is to be found in Section 1 (1), which provides that—

" Where a tenant of a holding has made thereon any improvement comprised in the First Schedule to this Act he shall, subject as in this Act mentioned, and, in a case where the contract of tenancy was made on or after the first day of January, nineteen hundred and twenty-one,[1] then whether the improvement was or was not an improvement which he was required to make by the terms of his tenancy, be entitled, at the termination of the tenancy, on quitting his holding to obtain from the landlord as compensation for the improvement such sum as fairly represents the value of the improvement to an incoming tenant."

The improvements comprised in the First Schedule are divided into Parts I, II and III, according as to whether the improvement is one in respect of which the consent of, or notice to the landlord is or is not required.

The following are the improvements which are included in Part I of the First Schedule :—

(1.) Erection, alteration, or enlargement of buildings.

(2.) Formation of silos.[2]

(3.) Laying down of permanent pasture.

(4.) Making and planting of osier beds.

(5.) Making of water meadows or works of irrigation.

(6.) Making of gardens.

(7.) Making or improvement of roads or bridges.

(8.) Making or improvement of watercourses, ponds, wells, or reservoirs, or of works for the application of water power or for supply of water for agricultural or domestic purposes.

---

[1] See *Huckell v. Saintey*, C.A., [1923] 1 K.B. 150.

[2] A *Silo* is a receptacle in which green fodder in its succulent condition is preserved, instead of first drying it into hay. The process of thus preserving fodder is called *ensilage*, the preserved material being called *silage*.

(9.) Making or removal of permanent fences.

(10.) Planting of hops.

(11.) Planting of orchards or fruit bushes.

(12.) Protecting young fruit trees.

(13.) Reclaiming of waste land.

(14.) Warping or weiring of land.[1]

(15.) Embankments and sluices against floods.

(16.) Erection of wirework in hop gardens.

(17.) Provision of permanent sheep-dipping accommodation.

(18.) In the case of arable land the removal of bracken, gorse, tree roots, boulders or other like obstructions to cultivation.

[N.B.—*This part is subject as to market gardens to the provisions of the Third Schedule.*][2]

With regard to the foregoing improvements, the Act[3] provides that compensation shall not be payable in respect of any of them, unless the landlord has, previously to the execution of such improvement, *consented* in writing to the making of the improvement, and any such consent may be given by the landlord unconditionally, or upon such terms as to compensation or otherwise as may be agreed upon between the landlord and the tenant; and if any such agreement is made any compensation payable thereunder shall be substituted for compensation under the Act. But, subject to the provisions of the Act, any contract (whether under seal or not) made by a tenant of a holding, by virtue of which his right to claim compensation under the Act is taken away or limited, is to that extent void.[4] The result would appear to be that a substituted agreement may only provide a different scale of compensation from that given by the Act. Accordingly, where a condition in a

---

[1] By *warping* is meant the covering of land with the sediment deposited from silt-laden streams or floods. The warp makes a rich top-dressing for the land.

[2] See p. 149 *et. seq, post.*

[3] Agricultural Holdings Act, 1923 s. 2.

[2] *Ibid.*, s. 50.

lease provided that no claim for compensation should be
made by the tenant later than one month prior to the
determination of the tenancy, whereas under the Act
then in force the tenant was entitled to make his claim
up to the last day of the tenancy, it was declared void.[3]

With regard to the improvement mentioned in Part
II of the First Schedule, [viz., *No.* 19 *" Drainage,"*]
it is provided that no compensation shall be payable
unless the tenant of the holding has not more than
three months and not less than two months before
beginning to execute such improvement, given written
notice to the landlord of his intention to make the same,
and of the manner in which he proposes to do the
intended work, and upon such notice being given, the
landlord and tenant may agree on the terms as to compensation or otherwise on which the improvement is to
be executed[2]; and if any such agreement is made, any
compensation payable thereunder shall be substituted
for compensation under the Act.[3]   In default of such
agreement the landlord may, unless the notice of the
tenant is previously withdrawn, execute the improvement in any reasonable and proper manner which he
thinks fit, and recover from the tenant, as rent, a sum
not exceeding 5 per cent. per annum on the outlay
incurred, or not exceeding such annual sum, payable
for a period of 25 years, as will repay that outlay in
that period, with interest at the rate of 3 per cent. per
annum; provided that, if the landlord fails to execute
the improvement within a reasonable time, the tenant
may execute the improvement, and shall, in respect
thereof, be entitled to compensation under the Act.[4]

---

[1] *Cathcart* v. *Chalmers*, [1911] A.C. 246.

[2] Agricultural Holdings Act, 1923 (13 & 14 Geo. 5, c. 9) s. 3 (1).

[3] *Ibid.*, s. 3 (2).

[4] *Ibid.*, s. 3 (3).

The following are the improvements included in Part III of the First Schedule, in respect of which consent of, or notice to the landlord is not required in order to entitle the tenant to compensation :—

(20.) Chalking of land.

(21.) Clay burning.

(22.) Claying of land or spreading blaes upon land.

(23.) Liming of land.

(24.) Marling of land.[1]

(25.) Application to land of purchased artificial or other purchased manure.

(26.) Consumption on the holding by cattle, sheep or pigs, or by horses other than those regularly employed on the holding, of corn cake, or other feeding stuff not produced on the holding.

(27.) Consumption on the holding by cattle, sheep, or pigs, or by horses other than those regularly employed on the holding, of corn proved by satisfactory evidence to have been produced and consumed on the holding.

(28.) Laying down temporary pasture with clover, grass, lucerne, sainfoin, or other seeds, sown more than two years prior to the determination of the tenancy.

(29.) Repairs to buildings, being buildings necessary for the proper cultivation or working of the holding, other than repairs which the tenant is himself under an obligation to execute:

Provided that the tenant, before beginning to execute any such repairs, shall give to the landlord notice in writing of his intention, together with particulars of such repairs, and shall not execute the repairs unless the landlord fails to execute them within a reasonable time after receiving such notice.

Upon the question of the amount of compensation payable, sub-sections (2) and (3) of Section 1 of the Act are important. They are as follows :—

" (2) In the ascertainment of the amount of the compensation payable to a tenant under this section there shall be taken into account—

" (a) any benefit which the landlord has given or allowed to the tenant in consideration of the tenant executing the improvement, whether expressly stated in the contract of tenancy to be so given or allowed or not; and

---

[1] Marl is clay containing variable quantities of carbonate of lime, and is put on to land either for the sake of the lime it brings with it, or on sandy soil on account of the clay it contains.

" (b) as respects manuring as defined by this Act, the value of the manure required by the contract of tenancy or by custom to be returned to the holding in respect of any crops grown on and sold off or removed from the holding within the last two years of the tenancy or other less time for which the tenancy has endured, not exceeding the value of the manure which would have been produced by the consumption on the holding of the crops so sold off or removed.

" (3) Nothing in this section shall prejudice the right of a tenant to claim any compensation to which he may be entitled under custom, agreement, or otherwise, in lieu of any compensation provided by this section.

The claim to compensation for improvements is restricted where they are begun by a tenant when about to quit his holding. By Section 8 :—

" A tenant of a holding shall not be entitled to compensation under this Act in respect of any improvements, other than manuring as defined by this Act, begun by him

" (a) in the case of a tenant from year to year, within one year before he quits the holding, or at any time after he has given or received notice to quit which results in his quitting the holding ; and

" (b) in any other case within one year before the termination of the tenancy :

" Provided that this section shall not apply in the case of any improvement—

" (i.) When the tenant, previously to beginning the improvement, has served notice on his landlord of his intention to begin it, and the landlord has either assented or has failed for a month after the receipt of the notice to object to the making of the improvement; or

" (ii.) In the case of a tenant from year to year, where the tenant has begun the improvement during the last year of his tenancy, and, in pursuance of a notice to quit thereafter given by the landlord, quits his holding at the expiration of that year.' '

CHAPTER XII.

LIABILITY FOR DAMAGE TO PERSON AND PROPERTY CAUSED BY DILAPIDATIONS.

PART 1.—INTRODUCTION.

In the previous chapters the circumstances have been discussed in which a man may, by virtue of estate, contract or statute, incur legal liability for the dilapidated state of buildings. A dilapidated building is often the cause of somebody suffering injury in his person or his property. Thus a rotten staircase may involve a broken leg, or a leaky roof cause damage to furniture. In this chapter it is proposed to describe the circumstances under which damage of this nature gives a right of action to the injured person. An important distinction must be borne in mind between the cases which have been discussed and those about to be discussed. In the former the dilapidated condition of the building directly gives rise to liability, whereas in the latter it is not the condition of the premises, but the injury caused thereby which gives rise to liability. Thus a shopkeeper may have a rotten staircase in his shop. As between himself and his landlord the condition of the stairs may involve him in legal liability under a repairing covenant in his lease. As between himself and his customers he is under no liability in respect of the staircase, although, as we shall see later, he may incur liability if one of his customers is hurt as a result of its condition.

The subject will be dealt with under the following heads :—

1. Liability of the occupier of premises to those who enter thereon.

2. Liability of the occupier of premises to persons using a high-way on which the premises abut.

10

3. Liability of the occupier of premises to neighbouring occupier.

4. Liability of owners of premises.

PART 2.—LIABILITY OF THE OCCUPIER OF PREMISES TO THOSE WHO ENTER THEREON.

If a third person coming or being upon premises is injured by reason of some disrepair thereof, the liability of the occupier in respect of such injury depends entirely on what legal duty is owed by him to the particular person who has been injured.

The person injured may have been a mere *trespasser*, *i.e.*, one who has no right on the premises at all, but who has come there unlawfully. To a trespasser the occupier owes no duty of care in regard to the condition of the premises. He may not, of course, shoot the trespasser at sight or assault or otherwise wilfully injure him, nor may he intentionally so arrange his premises that the trespasser shall be injured by mechanical means. In *Bird* v. *Holbrook*[1] the occupier, who had been much worried by trespassers, set a spring gun inside his walled garden with the intention that it should go off and injure anyone coming in. A neighbour, without the occupier's knowledge or consent, climbed the wall in search of a fowl which had strayed and was injured by the spring gun. It was held that he was entitled to recover damages for such injury from the occupier.

But this obligation not to injure the trespasser wilfully and intentionally is the limit of the occupier's duty toward such a person. He is, as stated above, under no duty to take any care as regards a trespasser to see that the premises are reasonably safe or to inform him of any dangerous spots in them.[2]

---

[1] 4 Bing. 628.

[2] See *Addie & Sons, Ltd.*, v. *Dumbreck*, 1929, A.C. 358 ; *Moulton* v. *Poulter*, 1930, The Times, Feb. 28th.

If the person coming upon the land is a *licensee,* the occupier does owe him a certain slight duty of care with respect to the condition of the premises. A licensee is one who is lawfully on the land with the consent, tacit or express, of the occupier. The class of licensees includes such persons as those tacitly permitted to cross the occupier's land, his social guests coming to the house, and in fact all persons lawfully coming on the land, but not being on business in which the occupier is himself interested. The duty owed by the occupier to such person is not to expose them to anything in the nature of a " concealed trap," *i.e.,* an unexpected danger on the premises which is known to the occupier, but which is not obvious to the licensee coming upon the premises.

In *Corby* v. *Hill*[1] an occupier of land had a private road for the use of persons coming to his house. He gave permission to a builder who was engaged in building on the land, to place materials upon this road. The builder placed a quantity of slates there, left them there at night and did not light them. The plaintiff drove along the road on his way to visit the occupier socially. He ran into the heap of slates and was injured. It was held that the occupier of the premises was liable as this heap of slates amounted to a " concealed trap."

In *Lowery* v. *Walker*[2] a farmer, who knew that people were in the habit of crossing his field and who acquiesced in the practice, put a horse which he knew to be savage in the field. The plaintiff while crossing the field was bitten by the horse, and it was held that this putting of a known savage horse there was in effect a concealed trap and made the farmer liable in damages to this licensee who was injured.

---

[1] 4 C.B. (N.S.) 556.
[2] [1911] A.C. 10.

Except as regards warning the licensee of anything in the nature of a concealed trap on the premises of which the occupier himself knows, there is no duty of care on him as regards licensees. He is not under any duty to take any care to find out any dangers; still less is he under any duty to licensees to keep the premises safe. In *Gautret* v. *Egerton*[1] the defendants owned certain land near some docks which they allowed persons coming to the docks to walk over. The land was intersected by a canal, across which there was a bridge. This bridge was in a bad state of repair. The plaintiff, going across the defendants' land on his way to the docks, fell through the bridge and was injured. It was held that the mere disrepair of the bridge gave a bare licensee no cause of action in respect of his injuries. Willes J. said, " The dedication of a permission to use the way (to the docks) must be taken to be in the nature of a gift. The principle of law as to gifts is that the giver is not responsible for damage resulting from the insecurity of the thing, unless he knew its evil character at the time, and omitted to caution the donee. There must be something like fraud on the part of the giver before he can be made answerable." " I cannot conceive that he (the defendant in this case) could incur any responsibility merely by reason of his allowing the way to be out of repair." This case has ever since been regarded as the leading case for the proposition that a bare licensee must take the premises as he finds them and that there is no liability on the occupier to do more than warn or protect him from any thing in the nature of a concealed trap of which the occupier knows.

This is the principle on which the so-called " staircase cases " turn. Nothing is commoner at the present day than for the owner of a house to let out suites

---

[1] L.R. 2 C.P. 371.

of rooms to various persons, but to retain the
staircase, corridors, roof, etc., under his own control and in his own occupation.   The owner of the
building is the occupier of the staircase, corridors
and roof, and the other persons coming upon the
premises to see the tenants of the various flats, whatever may be their relations to the various tenants, are,
as regards the owner of the building, merely bare
licensees. His only duty towards them therefore is not
to expose them to a concealed trap. This was finally
settled in the recent case of *Fairman* v. *Perpetual
Investment Building Society*,[1] overruling *Miller* v.
Hancock.[2] The defendant company owned a building
which they let out in flats but kept control of the staircase. The plaintiff was the sister-in-law of, and lodged
with the tenant of one of these flats. The stairs had
rods of iron embedded in the cement and the cement
had worn so that there was a hollow or depression in
the step just behind one of the iron bars. The plaintiff
had frequently used the staircase before, but on the
morning in question she caught her heel in the
depression and fell forward, suffering injuries. The
House of Lords was divided on the question of fact
involved in the case, two of the Law Lords thinking
that the condition of the step did amount to a concealed
trap and the other three being of a contrary opinion.
But they were unanimous in laying down the proposition
that the defendants' only duty to the plaintiff was not
to expose her to a concealed trap of which they, by
their servant, the caretaker, had knowledge.

It is difficult to see how the dilapidated condition of a
building can as a matter of practice constitute a trap,
and so involve the occupier in liability to a licensee;

[1] [1923] A.C. 74.
[2] [1893] 2 Q.B. 177.

for if the condition of the premises is obvious, there is no trap, and if it is not obvious it will be difficult to fix the occupier with knowledge of it, and knowledge of it is a necessary condition of liability. Suppose, for example, a house contains a wooden staircase, one of the treads of which becomes so rotten that a hole is worn in the woodwork, and suppose a licensee in using the staircase falls as a result of the hole and is injured. On the authority of *Fairman's* case (supra), it would seem that the licensee has no remedy, because, as the condition of the staircase is obvious, it does not constitute a trap. On the other hand, if this staircase, although in fact rotten, shows no sign of extraordinary wear until it suddenly gives way, it will be very difficult to establish knowledge on the part of the occupier. In short, the signs of decay necessary to give the occupier knowledge of the dilapidations will generally be sufficient to make it impossible for the licensee to say that the dilapidations are a trap.

In any case the liability of the occupier to a licensee is not a repairing liability. The occupier is under no duty to repair dilapidations in order to make the premises safe. His only duty is to warn licensees of hidden dangers (*i.e.*, dangers which would not be seen by a person using ordinary care) of which he knows either himself or through his agent.[1]

---

[1] There is some suggestion in the judgment of the House of Lords in *Fairman's* case that the duty extends to dangers of which the occupier ought to have known (see per *Lord Wrenbury*, (1923) A.C. p. 96). In *Sutcliffe* v. *Clients Investment Trust Company*, (1924) 2 K.B. 746, however, Bankes, L. J., referring to these expressions of opinion said at p. 755 "it was not necessary in that case" (*i.e.* in *Fairman's* case) "to enlarge the liability of an occupier towards a bare licensee, and it does not appear . . . . . that any of their Lordships intended to make any alteration in the Law . . . . . In my view this Court ought not to take those expressions as affecting any alteration in the Law." The better opinion, therefore, is that the occupier must have actual knowledge of the danger.

Finally, the person coming upon the premises may be an *invitee*. That is, he may be there on some business in which the occupier has an interest. As has been stated above, a social guest coming on the premises at the invitation of the occupier is a mere licensee and not one of the class which the law calls invitees. The converse is, however, true—that if he comes upon business he is, in the eyes of the law, an invitee, and it is immaterial whether he has been expressly invited in the ordinary sense of the word or not. The business need not be actual buying or selling or even such as will necessarily result in a contract; it is sufficient if it is business which concerns the occupier, or in which he is indirectly interested.

The occupier does not, even to invitees, guarantee the safety of the premises, but he does owe them a duty to take reasonable care not to expose them to any unusual danger of which he knows, *or which, if he had taken reasonable care, he would have known.*

The leading case on the subject is *Indermaur* v. *Dames*.[1] The plaintiff was a journeyman gasfitter. He was in the employ of a firm of gas-fitters who had supplied some burners to the defendant's sugar refinery. He was sent by his employers to the defendant's factory to test the burners. In the factory there was a shaft which was usual and necessary in sugar refineries. The shaft was, in fact, unfenced, although there was no reason why it could not be fenced when not actually working. Into this shaft the plaintiff fell, and in consequence thereof suffered injuries. He was held entitled to recover damages from the defendant, and the dictum of Willes, J. in this case has ever since been accepted as a correct statement of the law. Willes, J., after stating

---

[1] L.R. 1 C.P. 274 ; affd. 2 C.P. 311.

the facts, said that he had to deal with the law " as to the duty of an occupier of a building with reference to persons resorting thereto in the course of business, upon his invitation, express or implied." " And with respect to such a visitor at least, we consider it settled law, that he, using reasonable care on his part for his own safety, is entitled to expect that the occupier shall on his part *use reasonable care to prevent damage from unusual danger which he knows or ought to know.*"

So in *Sutcliffe v. Clients Investment Trust Co., Ltd.*,[1] the owners of a flat let it on lease to a tenant and agreed to contribute to the cost of decorating and repairing it at the beginning of the term. The tenant employed a firm of builders to do the work and, while doing it, the firm affixed an advertisement board to a balcony with a balustrade projecting from the front of the flat. It was held that the balcony did not form part of the leased premises, but was retained by the owner. A workman in the employ of the firm went on to the balcony to remove the board when the work was finished. The balustrade gave way and the man fell into the street and was killed. It was found as a fact that the balustrade was so dilapidated as to be dangerous, that the danger was not obvious to a person using the balcony with reasonable care and that the owners knew, or ought to have known of its condition. In an action by the widow of the dead man against the owners it was held that the workman was an invitee of the owners, because he was on the premises to do work in which they were interested, and because he was on a part of the premises which was in their occupation; and that, as they ought to have known of the dangerous state of the balcony, they were liable.

---

[1] (1924) 2 K.B. 746.

Finally there may be a contractual relationship subsisting between the occupier and the person on the premises, by virtue of which the latter pays for the privilege of entering, as where a man visits a theatre or restaurant, or stays in a hotel. In such cases the occupier impliedly warrants that the premises are as safe as reasonable care and skill can make them. If the other party to the contract is injured in person or property as a result of the dilapidated state of some part of the premises, the occupier will be liable unless he proves that the premises could not have been made safe by the exercise of reasonable care and skill.[1] He can not escape liability by showing that he did not know of, and could not by exercising due care have discovered the existence of the danger. In this respect an occupier owes a higher duty towards a person with whom he has made a contract of this kind than towards an invitee. Thus in *Maclenan* v. *Segar*[2] the plaintiff was injured as a result of fire which broke out in the defendant's hotel while she was staying there. The fire was caused by a defective scheme for conveying smoke and burning soot from the kitchen chimney. The defect was the result of negligence on the part of the architect or builder who had carried out the scheme. It was not definitely found by the jury that the defendant knew, or would have known had he been careful, of the existence of the danger. It was nevertheless held that he was liable. Had the plaintiff been an invitee, the defendant would not have been liable unless it could have been shown that he knew about the defective system, or was negligent in not knowing. Here again although the duty compels an occupier to make the

---

[1] The onus of proof will in most cases be on the occupier, for the fact of the injury will be *primâ facie* evidence of negligence.

[2] (1917) 2 K.B. 325.

premises safe, it does not necessarily involve him in the
execution of repairs to dilapidated parts of the premises.
The duty can obviously in many cases be discharged
by giving proper warning, by notice and lighting and
the like.

PART 3.—LIABILITY·OF AN OCCUPIER TO PERSONS USING A HIGHWAY ON WHICH THE PREMISES ABUT.

In the case of premises adjoining the highway the
occupier is liable to passers-by who may have been
injured by some defect in the premises, if such defect
either was due to the occupier's negligence or amounted
to a nuisance.

So, if a slate falls off the roof, or a chimney falls, or
glass falls out of window, whereby a passer-by is
injured, the occupier is liable if such accident happened
through any negligence on his part. Often, indeed,
the circumstances may be such that the injured party
need not in the first instance prove that the occupier
was negligent, for negligence will be presumed unless
and until the occupier proves the contrary which is
generally a very difficult thing to do. So in *Kearney*
v. *L.B. and S.C. Railway*[1] where a brick fell out of a
railway bridge, it was held that the mere happening
of the accident was sufficient *primâ facie* proof of the
negligence of the occupier.

If the disrepair of the premises amounts to a nuisance,
it does not make any difference that no part of it actually
impinges on the highway itself.

An exhaustive discussion of the law of nuisance is
outside the scope of this book. We are here only concerned with the circumstances in which a dilapidated
building may amount to a nuisance to a highway, and
so involve its occupier in legal liability. Broadly

---

[1] L.R. 6 Q.B. 759.

speaking premises are a nuisance to a highway if they are in a condition likely to cause injury to passers-by lawfully using the highway.   If, as a result of such a condition, a passer-by is injured the occupier will be liable for the injury in three cases :—[1]

(i) If he *causes* the nuisance, *e.g.,* by digging a hole on his land very close to the highway, into which a passer-by falls in the dark.   Obviously an occupier never causes a building to be in a dilapidated condition in this sense.

(ii) If by the neglect of some duty he *allows it to arise.* Thus it is the duty of an occupier of a house having an area fronting the public street so to fence it as to make it safe for persons using the highway.[2] If he fails to observe this duty by allowing the railings or fencing surrounding an area to fall into a state of disrepair, he will be liable if anyone is injured as a result.

In a recent case, one of the upright bars of an area railing to an empty house had been broken by boys playing football in the street, and a child got through the gap and was clambering along inside the railing when he fell and was injured.   It was held that the owner of the house was not liable for damages sustained in consequence of the alleged nuisance.   On appeal, the Court held that the alleged nuisance could not be regarded as the cause of the child's injuries, as he did not fall through the gap in the railings while using the highway, but got through the gap in order to clamber along inside.[3]

(iii) If, when it has arisen, he omits to remedy it within a reasonable time after he became aware of it (or would have become aware of it had he exercised reasonable care).   It is under this head that an occupier will be

[1] See *Noble* v. *Harrison*, (1926) 2 K.B. 332 at p. 338.

[2] *Coupland* v. *Hardingham*, (1813) 3 Camp. 398.

[3] *Barker* v. *Herbert*, [1911] 2 K.B. 633.

held liable if his building, or part of it, through dilapidations collapses into a highway and injures a passer-by. It must be observed that this liability is not absolute, that is to say the occupier is not in all circumstances liable if his building collapses into a highway and injures a passer-by, but only if he omits to shore up and repair the building within a reasonable time after he becomes aware of its dangerous condition or would have become aware of it had be exercised reasonable care by proper inspection and so on.   But, although theoretically the liability is not, it is submitted, absolute, a case can hardly be conceived in which an occupier could escape liability, for he cannot occupy a building and remain unaware that it is in danger of falling down unless he is grossly negligent, and as soon as he becomes aware of the danger he ought to take steps to guard against it.   "Within a reasonable time" in these cases would mean immediately.   In one case,[1] however, when part of the old city wall of Exeter collapsed into an abutting public house it was sought to make the owner liable. The Court held that the wall was not in the occupation of the owner, but of a weekly tenant of a cottage and garden of which the city wall was a retaining wall. The owner was held not liable and from the judgments it seems that an action framed against the occupying tenant would have been equally unsuccessful, because the tenant did not know and could not be expected to know that the wall, which had stood for centuries was dilapidated.   This was a case of damage to neighbouring property, but it is conceived that the same principles apply in the case of highways.

Where the thing which falls into the highway and causes the injury is something projecting over the

---

[1] *St. Anne's Well Brewery* v. *Roberts* 44 T.L.R. 703.

highway such as a lamp or clock, the liability of the occupier would seem to be absolute, and independent of any negligence or knowledge on his part. For example, where a heavy lamp, projecting over the footpath, fell and injured a foot passenger, the Court held that it was the tenant's duty to maintain the lamp so as not to be dangerous to the public, and, if it caused injury owing to want of repair, it was no answer on the part of the tenant that he had employed a competent and experienced gas-fitter to repair it and that the latter had been negligent.[1]

Finally, if an occupier brings on to his premises, or collects thereon anything which is likely to do damage if it escapes, he does so at his peril. " If it does escape and cause damage, he is responsible however careful he may have been, and whatever precautions he may have taken to prevent the damage." This is known as the rule in *Rylands* v. *Fletcher*,[2] the title of the case in which the rule was first laid down by the House of Lords. The rule is one of absolute liability. The occupier can only avoid it by showing that the escape of the agent which has caused the damage was brought about either by the act of the person complaining, or by an " act of God," that is by an intervention of extraordinarily violent or unusual natural causes (*e.g.*, an earthquake in England or a tremendously strong hurricane). For a complete discussion of the exact extent of the rule the reader is referred to the standard text books on the law of tort. For the purpose of the present book only two observations need be made.

(i) If an agent which is likely to do damage escapes from a building in which it is contained owing to some disrepair in the building, the occupier is liable for any

---

[1] *Tarry* v. *Ashton*, (1876) 1 Q.B.D. 314.

[2] *Rylands* v. *Fletcher*, L.R. 3 H.L. at p. 340.

consequential damage. The occupier of such a building must, therefore, insure that it is in such a state of repair as to prevent such an escape, and it will avail him nothing to say after an escape that he has taken reasonable care to make the building secure. Thus, if a person collects on his premises water in a reservoir, he must keep the walls of the reservoir in such a condition of repair as to prevent the water from escaping.

(ii) In *St. Anne's Well Brewery* v. *Roberts*,[1] referred to above, an attempt was made to apply the rule in *Rylands* v. *Fletcher* to buildings themselves. It was argued for the plaintiffs that the city wall was something likely to do damage if it escaped, that, when it collapsed, it did escape and that the occupier (the plaintiff submitted that the owner, the defendant, was in occupation) was liable apart from any question of whether he knew, or would have known had he been careful, of the state of the wall. This argument was rejected by the Court and it may, therefore, be taken as settled law that this rule of absolute liability has no application to damage caused by the collapse of dilapidated buildings.

PART 4.—LIABILITY OF OCCUPIER TO ADJOINING OWNERS.

We have seen that if an occupier suspends from his premises over a highway something such as a lamp or clock which falls and injures a passer-by, he is absolutely liable. An occupier has no right to suspend anything from his premises over his neighbour's land. If he does, he commits a trespass. In the former case, therefore, a right of action arises if and when a passer-by is injured. In the latter the adjoining owner has a right of action independent of injury.

[1] 44 T.L.R. 703.

Save in this respect the liability of an occupier to adjoining owners in respect of damage occasioned by dilapidations is the same as his liability to passers-by using an adjoining highway. That is to say :—

(i) He is liable for negligence.

(ii) He is liable when his premises become through dilapidations a nuisance, provided he knew of their condition or would have known of their condition had he exercised reasonable care, and has failed to remedy the condition within a reasonable time.

(iii) If he has collected or is keeping on his premises an agent which is likely to do damage if it escape, he is absolutely liable if the agent escapes and does damage through the disrepair of the building in which it is contained.

PART 5.—LIABILITY OF THE OWNER OF PREMISES.

So far in this chapter we have been considering the liability of the occupier for damage to person or property caused by the dilapidated state of the premises he occupies. We now turn to a discussion of the liability of the owner for such damage. Two preliminary observations may be made :—

1. If the owner is in occupation of the premises he is liable as occupier to the extent already described.

2. If the owner is not in occupation of the premises but has let them under a lease or tenancy agreement by which he undertakes repairing obligations, and if, as a result of his failure to carry out his obligations, damage is caused to the person or property of his tenant, the tenant can recover the loss he has sustained in an action on the repairing covenant.

For loss or damage caused to the person or property of anyone other than the tenant with whom he has contracted the owner who is not in occupation is generally speaking not liable. Thus in *Cavalier* v. *Pope*[1] the landlord contracted to repair the kitchen floor of the demised premises. He did not do so, and in consequence of its defective state the wife of the tenant was injured. It was held that she had no right of action against the landlord in respect of her injuries. This rule is only an application of the general principle of English law that no one can acquire rights by contract except the parties thereto. In the case just cited, the landlord's obligation to repair arose out of contract between himself and his tenant. Under that contract, the tenant's wife could not acquire any rights.

There is one exception to this rule in cases where the premises are through dilapidation in such a dangerous state as to be a nuisance. When this is so, the landlord is liable for all damage caused by the nuisance if, when he let them, he knew of their condition, or would have known had he exercised reasonable care.

Finally we must consider the extent of the obligation upon a landlord towards a tenant who has taken a lease of part of the premises, and who is injured as a result of some disrepair in the other part which the landlord has not let but has kept in his own control; as, for instance, when parts of a building are let in flats or chambers to different tenants, and the landlord keeps the remaining portions, including the foundations, roof, staircase, entrance hall, lifts, main drains, etc., under his control.

In a great many of the cases which have been decided where the tenant has suffered injury from the dilapidated condition of the stairs or the roof, the circumstances of the case are such that the landlord has been guilty of negligence in allowing them to get into

---

[1] (1905) 2 K.B. 575.

that state. It is therefore difficult to say whether the landlord has been held liable because of his tort of negligence or because he has committed a breach of some implied covenant to keep these parts of the building in repair. The cases seem more consistent with the view that the landlord is only liable when he has been guilty of negligence, but it must be admitted that the judges have frequently used language which seems to show that they put his liability on the ground of contract, *i.e.*, of an implied promise that he will keep his parts of the premises in repair.

Whether the duty be contractual or not it is quite clear that it is owed only to the tenant. With regard to third parties the landlord is liable as occupier of the reserved parts, and the extent of his liability as occupier is that described above. As we have seen, his duty is not a duty to repair or keep in repair, but merely one of keeping reasonably safe in the case of invitees[1] (a duty which can generally be adequately performed by warning against particular dangers); of warning against traps of which he actually knew in the case of licensees; and of not intentionally causing damage in the case of trespassers.

The extent of the landlord's duty towards the tenant is to take reasonable care to keep the retained parts of the building in a reasonably safe condition.

In *Dunster v. Hollis*,[2] Mr. Justice Lush decided that the law imposed an implied obligation on the landlord's part *to take reasonable care* to keep the staircase in a reasonably safe condition. This, of course, is nothing

---

[1] It must be noted that those who are *invitees quoad* the tenant when they reach the flat, are *licensees quoad* the landlord while using the stairs.

[2] [1918] 2 K.B. 795.

more than making the landlord liable for negligence, and it cannot make any difference whether it is put on the grounds of implied contract or of tort.

As regards the roof, in the case of *Hargroves, Aronson and Co.* v. *Hartopp*[1] the tenants occupied one floor in a building, and in consequence of a rain-water gutter on the roof (the possession and control of which was retained by the landlords) being stopped up, the water came in and damaged the tenants' goods. It was proved that the landlords never had the gutters or pipes examined or cleaned out, and that the rubbish which caused the stoppage was the accumulation of years. The tenants gave the landlords notice of the leakage, but they failed to have the gutter cleared out until after a lapse of four or five days from the receipt of the notice. The Court held that, as the gutter was under the control of the landlords, they were under a duty to take care that it was not in such a condition as to cause damage to the tenants, and, as they had received notice of its being stopped up and had neglected to clear it out within a reasonable time after the receipt of the notice, they were guilty of a want of due care and were consequently responsible for the damage done. It does not clearly appear whether the Divisional Court who tried the case put their decision on the ground of negligence or of implied contract, but it seems from Lord Alverstone's judgment that they decided the case as one of implied contract on the part of the landlord to use due care with regard to the premises.

In *Cockburn* v. *Smith*[2] the owner of a block of flats let one of the top flats to the plaintiff, but kept the roof and guttering in his own possession and control. The

---

[1] (1905) 1 K.B. 472.
[2] (1924) 2 K.B. 119.

guttering became defective, and rain water consequently entered the plaintiff's flat, and made it so damp
that she sustained injury to her health and suffered
damage. Mr. Justice Greer, after examining all the
authorities, came to the conclusion that the landlord's
duty and the tenant's correlative right rested on the
contract, express or implied, between them, and decided
that at any rate, if the parties had made (as in this case
they had) a contract in which the landlord expressly
agreed to repair some parts of the premises retained by
him, then *expressum facit cessare tacitum*, and he could
not be liable on any implied covenant to repair any other
part. On appeal, the Court of Appeal adopted the
position that the landlord had failed in the ordinary
common law duty to take due care and held him liable
for the damage on that ground. They refused to
decide the question of whether there was an implied
contractual duty apart from the duty to use care.

CHAPTER XIII.

SCHEDULING DILAPIDATIONS AND WASTE.

IN preparing a schedule of repairs, it is necessary to know, and a surveyor should inquire, whether the lease has expired, or whether it is continuing, in which case an " interim " schedule is required. He should also ascertain, by examining the lease, whether or not the landlord has reserved a right for himself or his agents to enter the premises for the purpose of viewing the state of repair, as without such a right the surveyor would be a trespasser, and before entering the premises it would be necessary to obtain permission from the tenant.

Even if the landlord has reserved the right to enter and view the state of repair, as a matter of courtesy it is usual for the surveyor to write and inform the tenant that he proposes doing so on a certain date, and asking whether that date will suit the convenience of the tenant.

In the case of houses coming within the provisions of the Housing, Town Planning, etc., Act, 1909, the landlord, or any person authorised by him, is entitled to enter such premises and view the state of repair at any reasonable time on giving twenty-four hours' notice to the tenant.

In determining questions of dilapidations it is necessary for the surveyor to bear in mind several practical considerations :—

(1.) He should first of all examine the lease or agreement, or a copy thereof. The repairing covenant should be carefully studied, and a note made as to what the tenant has agreed to do in the way of repairs.

(2.) The existence of any customs, local or otherwise. There is, for example, a custom in London, with regard to houses let for short terms of years, that the tenant should in no way be liable for external repairs, unless, of course, he has contracted to do them.

(3.) The character of the premises, their age and the class of neighbourhood in which they are situated.

(4.) The circumstances of the letting, *e.g.*, the age and condition of the premises at the time of letting, and any circumstances connected with the letting on which information can be obtained. Thus a tenant leasing old premises would, as a general principle, incur less liability than a tenant leasing new premises, and would, generally, only be required to keep them in repair *as old premises.*

(5.) If the covenant is to keep or to leave in " tenantable (or other similar expression) repair," what repairs will be necessary in order to satisfy a reasonably-minded incoming tenant of the class likely to take the premises.

(6.) If the lease is still running the surveyor should also ascertain whether he has a right to enter the premises, as already explained, and whether notice to repair has been given to the tenant in accordance with the provisions (if any) of the lease, and whether the time allowed therein for executing the repairs by the tenant has expired. In preparing a claim for dilapidations during the continuance of a lease, the damages should be measured by the amount of injury the reversion has sustained, owing to the failure to repair on the part of the tenant, as explained in Chapter VII.

(7.) In settling a claim for dilapidations a tenant may not set off the value of any improvements, except in the case of an agricultural tenancy.

In dealing with dilapidation questions in practice it is absolutely impossible to lay down any certain method of acquiring a knowledge of the work. Common sense, knowledge, tact, and a ready judgment are the first essentials. To these must be added years of practical experience. Take, for instance, the case of brickwork. The joints of the brickwork may be sound, but the wall itself bulged; on the other hand, the wall may be to all appearance perfectly straight and sound, but the pointing may, for all that, be decayed and perished, and the wall absolutely rotten. It may be asked what amount of bulging in a wall would justify a surveyor in requiring it to be taken down and rebuilt. In some cases, walls, say 30 feet in height, may be found over-hanging to the extent of nine inches or more, and yet so sound and well preserved that it would be most unfair to call upon the tenant to rebuild. In other cases, walls of equal height, overhanging not more than three inches, may be in such a condition as to call for rebuilding. In a very large percentage of cases it will be found necessary to require the top few courses of brickwork to be taken down and rebuilt! and in old buildings this almost invariably applies to parapet and party walls above the roof.

The point to be looked for—and it will be clearly apparent to the practical surveyor almost immediately he enters the premises to be surveyed—is whether the tenant has been a reasonably careful one, who has used the tenement fairly, and preserved it with a reasonable amount of reparation.

In inspecting the premises it is usual for surveyors to deal with the dilapidations in a certain order. The following is the order usually observed, and a descrip-tion of dilapidations to be looked for in each part of the premises is given :—

THE ROOF.

The chimney pots should be examined for the purpose of noting any cracked or broken pots or defective setting. The brickwork of chimney stacks, parapet walls and party walls should be carefully inspected, noting any brickwork out of upright or otherwise defective, together with any open or defective pointing to the brickwork. If any of the brickwork is rendered in cement, the condition of the rendering should be noted. The fall of the gutters, together with their condition, particular care being taken in observing the condition of any zinc work; if the fall of gutters is not correct it may generally be attributed to the sagging or decay of the wooden bearers. The condition of the lead cesspools should be noticed, also whether the gratings in outlets, or the wire covers (if any) are decayed. The slating, tiling, or other roof covering should be examined, the pointing of the tiles and the pointing at verges, etc., should be observed, slipped tiles or slates noted. Any sagging of the roof should be carefully noted; this, in some cases, may necessitate the complete restripping of the roof, the insertion of new rafters, etc. The condition of ridges, hips, valleys, hip irons, lead or zinc flashings, etc. Defective coping, broken stones, or defective cement work, particularly the condition of the cramps, should be looked to. The woodwork is often found to be decayed, more particularly that of skylights and trap-doors, these almost invariably being defective; likewise cistern tops, etc. Lastly, a note should be made of any paintwork.

It is often difficult to obtain access to the roof, and usually a very dirty job. It is, therefore, advisable for the surveyor when upon the roof, whether his instructions include the preparation of an estimate of the cost of repair or not, to insert in his notebook the various measurements which would be necessary to enable him to prepare such an estimate.

FRONT AND BACK OF HOUSE.

The condition of the brickwork, and whether bulged or not, the surveyor using his judgment as to when it is necessary to plumb the work; the condition of the pointings. It is usual in requiring re-pointing to note the style of this work, whether tuck-pointing, struck-pointing or whatever kind of pointing has been previously used. The pointing round the various windows and door openings should be particularly noted. The reveals, if cement, should be examined to ascertain whether they are sound or cracked, and if they have been previously painted. The condition of the various window sills. The general condition of the woodwork should next be noted. All stone steps, landings, etc., should be carefully examined; cracked and defective stones may require renewal, it often not being sufficient to have these cemented up. It may be necessary to consider whether cracks or defects are the result of settlement arising from inherent defects in the original construction of the building, and in such a case the question of the age and condition of the house at the commencement of the lease may arise. Defects to fences, gates, area walls, etc., should be noted; almost invariably garden walls will be found faulty. The condition of rain-water and soil-pipes, eaves-gutters, outside shutters, sun blinds, etc., should be noted. Lastly, the condition of the outside paintwork should be recorded.

INTERNAL WORK.

It is usual to commence on the top floor of the house and work down to the basement. Each room is taken in succession, starting with the roof on the left of the staircase and working " sun-wise," *i.e.,* from left to right, and the rooms should be dealt with in the same order, as nearly as may be, on each floor. The work in each room should be noted systematically, viz., the ceiling, whether the plastering is bulged, badly cracked, or in any other way defective; if very bad it may be necessary to investigate the condition of the lathing. Also the cornices should be noted. Usually the formula, " wash, stop, claircolle and whiten ceiling " will be found sufficient. Often the ceiling will have been papered to hide defects. If an estimate is being prepared and measurements taken, the ceiling should be measured first and booked, since the length and breadth of it added together and multiplied by two will give the girth of the room, which multiplied by the height, will give the gross area of the walls for papering, from which figure deductions are afterwards made for the door, window, and fireplace openings as each one is measured. Next the walls should be examined, noting the condition of the plastering, and also if the paper has been torn, or merely soiled. The window sashes and frames should be next examined, noting defective woodwork, broken sash lines, missing or defective fastenings, broken glass and faulty puttying. Next, the condition of the flooring, if of wood, whether it is worn or broken, noting any sagging of the joists. The skirting and other woodwork, whether defective or decayed, and, if the latter, whether resulting from neglect to paint. The effects of dry rot should be carefully looked for, particularly in basement houses. This is attributable to the formation and growth of species of fungi. The cause, or perhaps it is more correct to say the condition essential to the development of this growth, is neglect to ventilate under the floors, and points to faulty original construction, which however, can sometimes be remedied by the insertion of air bricks. Wet rot, on the other hand, is the result of a chemical decomposition, and its existence is clearly the result of permissive waste. Mantelpieces should be carefully inspected for cracks and chipping; and if of marble, whether pickling and cleaning are required. The condition of the front and back hearths, whether broken or otherwise defective. The condition of the stove or stoves. Lastly, the state of the paint-work. On leaving each floor it is usual to deal with the staircase leading from that floor, together with the landing, taking in order the ceilings and the soffits, then the walls, following with a note of the condition of the handrail, balusters, etc., the treads and risers, noting whether worn or otherwise defective, faulty strings or other woodwork. Note the state of windows on landings, etc., as also the doors of cupboards, etc., with the external faces of room doors.

See that keys are not missing, and whether door furniture is defective or needs relacquering. Try the electric and other bells, speaking-tubes, etc., and see if in working order.

Examine the bath, lavatory, and w.c. fittings. Try the water-waste-preventers (if the water is still laid on), and notice any cracks or other defects. Also the storage cisterns, whether it will be necessary to clean them out; the condition of the ball valves, etc. If the bath waste discharges into a rain-water head, see if choked with bird's nests, etc., and whether new gratings are required.

DRAINS.

The condition of the drains should be carefully examined, noting defective gullies and sanitary fittings, as also indications of defects in the soil drains. If any indications of defects exist it is justifiable to call upon the tenant to open and examine the drains, repairing and cleansing the same if requisite. Most surveyors insert a clause in their schedules calling for this to be done, whether any defects are indicated or not; but they rarely get all they ask for. The manhole covers can sometimes be lifted up, and some slight idea as to the condition of the drains can, in this way, be obtained.

APPENDIX.

APPENDIX.

THE FIRES PREVENTION (METROPOLIS) ACT, 1774.[1]
(14 GEO. III., c. 78.)

An Act for the further and better Regulation of Buildings and Party Walls, and for the more effectually preventing Mischiefs by Fire within the Cities of London and Westminster, etc.

SECTION. 83.—" And in order to deter and hinder ill-minded persons from wilfully setting their house or houses, or other buildings, on fire with a view of gaining to themselves the insurance money, whereby the lives and fortunes of many families may be lost or endangered "; be it further enacted, that it shall and may be lawful to and for the respective governors or directors of the several insurance offices for insuring houses or other buildings against loss by fire, and they are hereby authorized and required upon the request of any person or persons interested in or entitled unto any house or houses, or other buildings, which may hereafter be burnt down, demolished, or damaged by fire, or upon any grounds of suspicion that the owner or owners, occupier or occupiers, or other person or persons who shall have insured such house or houses, or other buildings, have been guilty of fraud, or of wilfully setting their house or houses, or other buildings, on fire, to cause the insurance money to be laid out and expended, as far as the same will go, towards rebuilding, reinstating or repairing such house or houses, or other buildings so burnt down, demolished, or damaged by fire; unless the party or parties claiming such insurance money shall, within sixty days next after his, her, or their claim is adjusted, give a sufficient security to the governors or directors of the insurance office where such house or houses, or other buildings, are insured, that the same insurance money shall be laid out and expended as aforesaid; or unless the said insurance money shall be, in that time settled and disposed of to and amongst all the contending parties to the satisfaction and approbation of such governors or directors of such insurance office respectively.

---

[1] This Act was originally referred to as the Metropolitan Building Act, 1774, but under the Short Titles Act, 1896, is now cited as above.

86.—And be it further enacted, that no action, suit, or process whatever shall be had, maintained, or prosecuted against any person in whose house, chamber, stable, barn, or other building, or on whose estate any fire shall, after the said 24th day of June (1774), accidentally begin, nor shall any recompense be made by such person for any damage suffered thereby; any law, usage, or custom to the contrary notwithstanding. And, in such case, if any action be brought, the defendant may plead the general issue, and give this Act and the special matter in evidence, at any trial thereupon to be had; provided that no contract or agreement made between landlord and tenant shall be hereby defeated or made void.

[NOTE.—It appears to have been the intention of the Legislature to repeal both Sections 83 and 86 of the above Act.[1]

These sections, with certain others, were kept in force by Section 109 of the Metropolitan Buildings Act, 1855.[2] By Section 34 of the Metropolitan Fire Brigade Act, 1865,[3] the other sections were repealed, leaving Sections 83 and 86 alone in force.

By the Statute Law Revision Act, 1875[4] (Schedule), both Section 109 of the Metropolitan Buildings Act, 1855, and Section 34 of the Metropolitan Fire Brigade Act, 1865 (*i.e.*, the sections of the Acts which kept Sections 83 and 86 of 14 Geo. III., c. 78, in force), were specifically repealed. As, however, Section 1 of the Statute Law Revision Act, 1875, provides that " where any enactment not comprised in the Schedule has been repealed, confirmed, revised or perpetuated by any enactment hereby repealed, such repeal, confirmation, revivor or perpetuation shall not be affected by this Act," and since both Section 109 of the Metropolitan Buildings Act, 1855, and Section 34 of the Metropolitan Fire Brigade Act, 1865, were a " confirmation or perpetuation " of Sections 83 and 86 of 14 Geo. III., c. 78, and the latter enactment was not included in the Schedule of the Statute Law Revision Act, 1875, the result appears to be that both Sections 83 and 86 of 14 Geo. III., c. 78, are still in force, and that the inclusion of the above-mentioned sections in the Schedule was futile.]

---

[1] 14 Geo. III., c. 78.

[2] 18 & 19 Vict , c. 122.

[3] 28 & 29 Vict., c. 90.

[4] 38 & 39 Vict., c. 66.

THE HOUSING ACT, 1925.

(15 Geo. V., c. 14.)

An Act to consolidate the enactments relating to the Housing of the Working Classes in England and Wales.

[*9th April, 1925.*

1.—(1) In any contract for letting for habitation a dwelling house at a rent not exceeding :—

(*a*) in the case of a house situate in the administrative county of London, forty pounds;

(*b*) in the case of a house situate elsewhere, twenty-six pounds; there shall, notwithstanding any stipulation to the contrary, be implied a condition that the house is at the commencement of the tenancy, and an undertaking that the house will be kept by the landlord during the tenancy, in all respects reasonably fit for human habitation : Provided that the condition and undertaking aforesaid shall not be implied when a house is let for a term of not less than three years upon the terms that it be put by the lessee into a condition reasonably fit for habitation, and the lease is not determinable at the option of either party before the expiration of three years.

(2) The landlord, or any person authorised by him in writing, may at reasonable times of the day, on giving twenty-four hours' notice in writing to the tenant or occupier, enter any premises to which this section applies for the purpose of viewing the state and condition thereof.

(3) In this section the expression " landlord " means any person who lets for habitation to a tenant any house under any contract referred to in this section, and includes his successors in title, and the expression " dwelling-house " includes part of a dwelling house.

2.—(1) Notwithstanding any agreement to the contrary, when under any contract of employment of a workman employed in agriculture the provision of a house or part of a house for the occupation of the workman forms part of the remuneration of the workman, and the provisions of the foregoing section are inapplicable by reason only of the house or part of a house not being let to the workman, there shall be implied as part of the contract of employment, the like condition and undertaking as would be implied under those provisions if the house or part of the house were so let, and those provisions shall apply accordingly as if incorporated in this section, with the substitution of " employer " for " landlord," and such other modifications as may be necessary.

3.—(1) If the owner of any dwelling-house suitable for occupation by persons of the working classes fails to make and keep the house in all respects reasonably fit for human habitation, then, without prejudice to any other powers, the local authority may serve a notice upon the owner of the house requiring him within a reasonable time, not being less than twenty-one days, specified in the notice, to execute the works specified in the notice as being necessary to make the house in all respects reasonably fit for human habitation :

Provided that, if such house is not capable without re-construction of being rendered in all respects reasonably fit for human habitation, the owner may, within twenty-one days after the receipt of such notice, by written counter-notice to the local authority declare his intention of closing the house for human habitation, and thereupon a closing order shall be deemed to have become operative in respect of the house. Any question arising under this proviso shall, in case of difference between the owner and the local authority, be determined by the Minister.

(2) If the notice of the local authority is not complied with, then—

(*a*) at the expiration of the time specified in that notice if no such counter-notice as aforesaid has been given by the owner ; and

(*b*) at the expiration of twenty-one days from the determination by the Minister if such notice has been given by the owner, and the Minister has determined that the house is capable without reconstruction of being made in all respects reasonably fit for human habitation ;

the local authority may themselves do the work required to be done.

(3) Any expenses incurred by the local authority under this section, together with interest at such a rate as the Minister may, with the approval of the Treasury, from time to time by order fix, from the date of service of a demand for the same till payment thereof from the owner, may be recovered in a court of summary jurisdiction and until recovery of such expenses and interest the same shall be a charge on the premises. In all

summary proceedings by the local authority for the recovery of any such expenses, the time within which the proceedings may be taken shall be reckoned from the date of the service of notice of demand.

(8) In addition to serving the notice on the owner, the local authority may serve copies of the notice on any persons having an estate or interest in the premises superior to that of the owner, and it shall be the duty of the owner or any other person having such an estate or interest, on being so required by the local authority, to state the name and address of the person from whom he holds, and if he fails to do so, or knowingly makes a mis-statement, he shall be liable on summary conviction to a fine not exceeding five pounds.

4.—Where a house in respect of which a notice has been served upon the owner by the local authority under subsection (1) of the past foregoing section is not capable without reconstruction of being rendered in all respects reasonably fit for human habitation, and a closing order has in consequence been deemed to have become operative in respect thereof, the Minister may on the application of the local authority make an order authorising the authority to acquire the house, and thereupon this Act shall apply as if the house where land authorised to be acquired compulsorily for the purposes of a reconstruction scheme under Part II. of this Act, and that land had been included in the scheme on account of the sanitary condition of the premises thereon.

ECCLESIASTICAL DILAPIDATIONS MEASURE, 1923, AS AMENDED BY THE ECCLESIASTICAL DILAPIDATIONS (AMENDMENT) MEASURE, 1929.

3.—In this measure :—

The term " Central Authority " shall mean Queen Anne's Bounty ;

The term " Diocesan Dilapidations Board " (hereinafter sometimes called " the Board ") shall mean the Diocesan Dilapidations Board constituted under the provisions of this Measure, and where referred to in connection with a particular benefice shall mean the Diocesan Dilapidations Board for the area in which such benefice is situated ;

12

The term " Diocesan Conference " shall mean the Diocesan
Conference of a diocese constituted as provided in the
Regulation passed by the National Assembly of the
Church of England, and known as the Diocesan Confer-
ences Regulation, 1922;

The term " benefice " shall include all rectories with cure
of souls, vicarages, perpetual curacies, separate districts
for spiritual purposes formed under the New Parishes Act,
1843, endowed public chapels and parochial chapelries, and
chapelries or districts belonging or reputed to belong, or
annexed or reputed to be annexed, to any church or
chapel;

4.—(2) The provisions of this Measure respecting buildings
belonging to a benefice shall apply to all such houses of residence,
glebe buildings, walls, fences, and other buildings and things as
the incumbent of the benefice is by law or custom bound to
maintain in repair, and the drainage thereof and the supply of
water thereto, but shall not apply to churches or chancels save
as hereinafter expressly provided.

9.—(1) As soon as possible after the passing of this Measure
the Diocesan Conference of each diocese shall frame a scheme
for the constitution of a Diocesan Dilapidations Board for the
whole diocese, or, if the Conference resolve for the purposes of
this Measure to divide the diocese into parts, then for the constitution of a Board for each part.

(2) The scheme shall determine the number of the members
of each Board, and the method of choosing them, and all other
matters necessary for the proper constitution of each Board.

12.—(1) The Board when constituted shall appoint such fit
persons as Surveyors as may be required for the purposes of this
Measure. Each appointment shall be for a term not exceeding
five years, and may be for the whole or such part of the diocese
or other area administered by the Board as the Board shall
determine and as shall be stated in the appointment. If more
than one Surveyor be appointed for any area, the Board may, if
it thinks fit, from time to time determine which of such surveyors
shall ordinarily act in respect to each benefice in the area.

(2) Any surveyor whose appointment shall lapse by effluxion
of time or otherwise than by removal from office as hereinafter
provided shall be entitled to act for the purposes of this Measure
until a successor shall be appointed.

(3) Every Surveyor shall be under the control and direction of the Board by which he was appointed.

(4) Any complaint against the Surveyor for neglect or breach of duty or misconduct shall be made to the Board, who, after giving him opportunity of showing cause to the contrary, shall have power to remove him from his office.

(5) No Surveyor appointed under the provisions of this Measure shall have any claim to compensation on account of any such compulsory removal as aforesaid or of any repeal or alteration of this Measure.

(6) On a vacancy occurring in the office of Surveyor, a fit person may be appointed by the Board as soon as possible after the occurrence of the vacancy.

(7) A Surveyor shall be paid according to a scale of fees or by salary fixed by the Board; and the scale of fees or salary may from time to time be revised by the Board but not so as to affect the remuneration of a Surveyor in respect to any work then already done or in course of being done by him.

14. It shall not be lawful for the Surveyor to be beneficially interested directly or indirectly, by himself or by any partner or otherwise, in any work or contract to be executed or entered into by any person or persons (except any public company of which he may happen to be a member or shareholder, but not manager or director), under the provisions of this Measure : Provided that nothing herein contained shall prevent the Surveyor being employed and paid by the incumbent either as architect or otherwise to supervise the execution of the works.

15.—(1) It shall be lawful for any Surveyor employed under this Measure, and for his servants and workmen, and for any person authorised by or on behalf of the Board for the purposes of this Measure, at all reasonable hours during the daytime, from time to time after due notice to the incumbent (if any), to enter into the buildings belonging to any benefice and to inspect and examine the same, and also any works in progress under this Measure.

(2) Where by reason of the refusal or neglect of the person responsible for the dilapidations any repairs are required under this Measure to be executed or buildings to be reinstated, it shall be lawful, after due notice, for all persons authorised by the Surveyor to enter into the buildings belonging to such benefice and to execute the works so required to be executed.

17.—(1) As soon as a Diocesan Dilapidations Board shall have been constituted, the Board shall cause first inspections to be made for the purposes of this Measure of all the buildings of each benefice in the diocese or area for which it has been constituted.

(2) Such first inspections shall be made within a period of seven years from the passing of this Measure in such order, in respect to the benefices in its area, as the Board may in its discretion determine, and in so determining the Board shall have due regard to the dates of inspections made and of certificates (if any) registered under the preceding Acts : Provided that upon any benefice becoming vacant or being placed under sequestration, the buildings belonging to such benefice, in respect of which no first inspection shall have been made, shall be inspected forthwith.

18.—(1) On each inspection of the buildings of a benefice made under section 17 of this Measure the Surveyor shall make a report to the Board based on the obligation on the person lawfully bound to keep or have kept such buildings in good and substantial repair, and stating—

" (i) whether any and, if so what immediate repairs are needed, specifying the same in detail together with their estimated cost ;

(ii) except in respect of dilapidations caused by the deliberate action or gross neglect of an incumbent, within what time not exceeding twelve months such immediate repairs as are needed should be carried out;

(iii) what sum will, in his opinion and upon the assumption that such immediate repairs as are needed will be duly carried out, be required to meet the probable cost of the repairs (in this Measure referred to as " the quinquennial repairs ") which will require to be carried out during the five years immediately succeeding the date of his report;

(iv) what sum, if any, in addition to the sums respectively required to meet the cost of such immediate repairs as are needed and the quinquennial repairs respectively, will be required to meet the probable cost of any future repairs (in this Measure referred to as " deferred repairs ") for the carrying out of which during a period exceeding five years from the date of his report it is, in his opinion, desirable to provide a fund;

(v) the general character of any deferred repairs to which his report relates, the reasons for their classification as such, and within what time they should be carried out;

(vi) what sum, in his opinion, will be adequate to reinstate each of such buildings in the event of its being destroyed by fire; and, if the Diocesan Dipalidations Board shall so require;

(vii) whether any and, if so, which of such buildings is in his opinion unsuitable to the needs of the benefice, and what sum would, in his opinion, be required to provide a building adequate to the needs of the benefice in the place of any unsuitable building."

(2) The Surveyor shall forthwith send a copy of such report to—

(i) the incumbent of the benefice; and

(ii) in case of the sequestration of a benefice, to the sequestrator; and

(iii) in the case of a first inspection, to any previous incumbent of the benefice not protected under section five of this Measure, or his executors or administrators.

(3) The copy of each report shall be accompanied by copies of section 20 and sub-section (1) of section 21 of this Measure and a notice addressed to the person to whom a copy of this report is sent that he may, if he so desires, send to the Board within twenty-one days a tender for the execution of the work or any part of it.

(4) The Surveyor shall certify to the Board when and to whom and in what manner such copies and notices shall have been sent.

20.—(1) Within one month from the sending of a copy of the report of the Surveyor under this Measure to the person sought to be made responsible for dilapidations in accordance with the provisions of this Measure, whether for the execution of the repairs or for any payment in respect of them, such person may object to the report in writing to the Board on any grounds of fact or law.

21.—(1) If no objection be made, then on the expiration of one month from the sending of the copy of a report as aforesaid, or if objection be made, then so soon as the Board shall have determined upon every such objection, the Board shall make an order confirming the report of the Surveyor without variation or with such variation as the Board may in its discretion decide.

(2) The order of the Board so made shall state the estimated cost of the immediate repairs, the time within which such repairs are to be carried out, and the name of any person who under the provisions of this Measure is liable to make any payment to the Central Authority in respect of such repairs or any part thereof, and in the case of a first inspection shall require payment of such estimated cost from any person from whom such payment is due.

22.—(1) When under section 17 of this Measure there is a first inspection of the buildings belonging to a benefice, if it be on the occasion of a vacancy in the benefice and the late incumbent is not protected by a certificate, then the late incumbent or his executors or administrators, and if it be not on the occasion of a vacancy, then the incumbent (or in the case of a sequestration, the sequestrator) shall pay to the Central Authority the sum required to be paid in the order made under section 21 of this Measure in respect to the cost of the immediate repairs to the buildings of the benefice estimated in accordance with section 18 of this Measure.

(2) The sum shall be due to be paid as from the date of the order and shall be a debt due to the Central Authority from the person responsible or his estate, and shall be recoverable as such at law.

24.—(1) As soon as may be after receiving a copy of the order of the Board under section 21 of this Measure the Central Authority shall make an Ordinary Assessment fixing for the next quinquennial period an annual payment to be made on account of the buildings to which the order of the Board relates.

(2) The annual payment to be fixed by such Ordinary Assessment shall consist of—

(i) a sum (in this Measure called " the Repair Rate ") sufficient in the opinion of the Central Authority to meet the estimated cost of the repairs required by the order of the Board made under section 21 of this Measure, except

(a) repairs of which the cost is spread over more than five years under section 26 of this Measure, and

(b) repairs required under section 19 of this Measure in respect to wilful dilapidations, and

(c) repairs the cost of which is required by the order of the Board to be paid in consequence of a first inspection under section 17 of this Measure or is otherwise provided for ;

(ii) a further sum (in this Measure called " the Insurance Rate ") in respect to the insurance premium necessary to provide the capital sum fixed by the order of the Board under section 21 of this Measure in pursuance of the report of the Surveyor under section 18 of this Measure as being adequate to reinstate the buildings if destroyed by fire;

(iii) such further sum (if any) (in this Measure called " the Administration Rate ") as the Central Authority shall determine to be the necessary and proper contribution from the benefice towards the administrative expenses of the Central Authority and of the Board (including salaries or fees of Surveyors).

25.—(1) The first annual payment required by the first Ordinary Assessment made in respect to buildings belonging to a benefice shall be due from the incumbent or sequestrator of the benefice to the Central Authority at the expiration of twelve months from the date of such assessment: Provided that the Central Authority may, if they think fit, substitute for twelve months any period not less than nine months nor more than fifteen months from the date of such assessment, and in that case payment shall be due at the expiration of such substituted period.

(2) Subsequent annual payments required by the first Ordinary Assessment shall be due from the incumbent or sequestrator to the Central Authority at equal intervals of twelve months beginning from the date fixed for the first payment in accordance with the preceding subsection and continuing for four years from such date until the end of the first quinquennial period.

(3) Annual payments fixed by any subsequent Ordinary Assessment shall be in like manner due to the Central Authority at equal intervals of twelve months for the succeeding period of five years; and the first payment required by any such subsequent Ordinary Assessment shall become due at the expiration of twelve months from the date at which the last payment required by the next preceding assessment became due: Provided that the Central Authority may, if they think fit, vary the date on which a first payment under a subsequent Ordinary Assessment shall become due in the same manner as is prescribed in the first subsection of this section in respect to the first payment required by the first Ordinary Assessment.

26.—(1) When any repairs are included in the report of the Surveyor as deferred repairs, not being repairs of which the cost has been otherwise provided for, and the Board shall be of opinion that the cost of them should be spread over a period longer than five years, the Board shall so inform the Central Authority, and the Central Authority shall thereupon make an assessment (in this Measure called a " Long Assessment ") similar to an Ordinary Assessment under Section 24 of this Measure except that the payments required shall be spread over such a period longer than five years as the Board shall think reasonable.

The annual payments required by a Long Assessment shall be a charge on the revenues of the benefice having such priority in respect to other charges as is in this Measure prescribed, and the provisions of section 25 in regard to an Ordinary Assessment and to the powers of the Central Authority shall apply with the necessary modifications and so far as applicable as though a Long Assessment were substituted for an Ordinary Assessment in that section.

29. The repair rate paid in respect of a benefice shall be placed by the Central Authority to the credit of an account to be called the ' Repair account of the benefice of   ,' and they shall allow interest thereon at such rate and on such terms and conditions as they may from time to time determine, and credit the same to the account.

31.—(1) It shall be the duty of an incumbent of a benefice not under sequestration to execute the repairs, including reinstatement of buildings destroyed by fire, required by any order of the Board in accordance with such order and with the provisions of this Measure and in particular within the time prescribed by the Board under those provisions.

(3) Provided always, that there shall be no obligation on the part of the sequestrator of a benefice under this section to execute any ordinary or structural repairs the cost of which exceeds the sums for the time being standing to the credit of the Ordinary Repair Account and of the Deferred Repair Account of the benefice respectively; and the obligation of the incumbent to execute ordinary or structural repairs shall in like manner not exceed such sums as aforesaid with the addition of such sums (if any) as may be due from the incumbent to the Central Authority, and payable to such accounts respectively.

(6) If the incumbent of a benefice who is required under this Measure to execute repairs shall refuse or neglect to execute them, the Board may represent his default to the Bishop, and thereupon the Bishop may, if he think fit, issue sequestration of the benefice; and it shall then be the duty of the sequestrator to execute the repairs as in this section provided.

32.—(1) The sums standing to the credit of the Ordinary Repair Account and the Structural Repair Account respectively of a benefice shall be available for the appropriate repairs of the buildings belonging to the benefice, being repairs included in an order of the Board made under Section 21 of this Measure.

(3) When the repairs in respect to which disbursements are required have been completed, the Surveyor shall in giving his certificate so inform the Board and the Central Authority; and if such repairs shall have not been completed by reason of the insufficiency of the money available to complete them the Surveyor shall so inform the Board and the Central Authority, and shall certify to the Central Authority the total amount required in respect to the repairs, stating separately the amount required for work already done and the amount required for work still to be done in order to complete the repairs; and upon receipt of such certificate duly countersigned as aforesaid, the Central Authority may disburse the total amount required for the work which has been done.

46.—(1) If a Surveyor, when he is making a report under this Measure, shall be of opinion that any building belonging to a benefice is superfluous, he shall report to the Board accordingly; and an incumbent may represent to the Board that any building belonging to his benefice is superfluous; and after receiving any such report or representation, the Board may in its descretion, with the consent of the patron and incumbent, order the removal of such building and the sale of its materials.

(2) Any surplus proceeds of such removal (after all expenses have been paid) shall be paid to the Central Authority, who shall apply the same, in accordance with the provisions of Section 47 of this Measure.

47. If any buildings belonging to a benefice shall by sale or removal with the proper sanctions cease to belong to the benefice, and there shall remain any sum standing to the credit either of the Ordinary Repair Account or the Structural Repair Account of the benefice in respect of those buildings, it shall be lawful

for the Central Authority with the consent of the Board to apply such sum (or any part thereof) at their discretion for any one or more of the following purposes—

    (i) the improvement of any buildings belonging to the benefice;

    (ii) the augmentation of the benefice;

    (iii) the discharge of any charge made on the revenues of the benefice by a Charging Assessment under this Measure or the payment of the interest on such charge;

    (iv) the repayment of the sum to the incumbent (or his executors or administrators) or the sequestrator by whom such sum shall have been contributed as required by this Measure.

52.—(1) As from the passing of this Measure there shall be no obligation on any incumbent to repair or insure the chancel of the church of the parish of which he is incumbent, if he be an incumbent who by reason only of his incumbency is rector of such parish or otherwise solely liable for such repair or insurance, and such chancel shall in all respects be repairable and insurable in the same manner as the remainder of such church.

INDEX.

INDEX.

FIRE
    covenant to rebuild in case of, 33
    damage caused by accidental is not waste, 6
               covered by covenant to repair, 94
               effect of exception of, 95
    landlord's liability to rebuild after, 95
    liability for damage caused by, 93
    policy of insurance against, 96

FIRES PREVENTION (METROPOLIS) ACT, 1774
    provisions of, 94
    text of, 173

FIT FOR HUMAN HABITATION
    implied condition that premises are, 98
        undertaking that premises will be kept, 98

FORFEITURE
    landlord's right of, 83
    notice before, effect of acceptance of rent on, 89
       by landlord before, form of, 88
    relief from, 85
    service of notice by landlord before, 85

HIGHWAY
    nuisance near, liability of occupier for, 155
    person using, liability of occupier to, 154

HOLDING OVER
    distinguished from fresh agreement, 71
    effect of, on covenant to repair, 69

HOUSE
    furnished, obligation of landlord on letting of, 23
    unfurnished, no obligation on landlord to repair, 21

HOUSING ACT, 1925
    condition and undertaking implied by, 98
    text of sections of, 175

HOUSING ACT, 1930, 111

IMPROVEMENTS
    authorised under the Settled Land Act, 11
    compensation to tenant for, 139
    under Agricultural Holdings Act, what are, 140

13